BELLA'S
Beautiful Miracle

A CATERPILLAR'S JOURNEY

Kimberly Novak

Trilogy Christian Publishers
A Wholly Owned Subsidiary of Trinity Broadcasting Network
2442 Michelle Drive
Tustin, CA 92780

Copyright © 2022 by Kimberly Novak

Scripture quotations marked BSB are taken from The Holy Bible, Berean Study Bible, BSB. Copyright ©2016, 2018 by Bible Hub. Used by Permission. All Rights Reserved Worldwide. www.berean.bible. Scripture quotations marked ESV are taken from the ESV® Bible (The Holy Bible, English Standard Version®), copyright © 2001 by Crossway Bibles, a publishing ministry of Good News Publishers. Used by permission. All rights reserved. Scripture quotations marked NIV are taken from the Holy Bible, New International Version®, NIV®. Copyright © 1973, 1978, 1984, 2011 by Biblica, Inc.TM Used by permission of Zondervan. All rights reserved worldwide. www.zondervan.com. The "NIV" and "New International Version" are trademarks registered in the United States Patent and Trademark Office by Biblica, Inc.TM. Scripture quotations marked NKJV are taken from the New King James Version®. Copyright © 1982 by Thomas Nelson. Used by permission. All rights reserved. Scripture quotations marked NLT are taken from the Holy Bible, New Living Translation, copyright © 1996, 2004, 2015 by Tyndale House Foundation. Used by permission of Tyndale House Publishers, Inc., Carol Stream, Illinois 60188. All rights reserved. Scripture quotations marked NOG are taken from The Names of God Bible (without notes) © 2011 by Baker Publishing Group. Used by permission of Baker Publishing Group. All rights reserved. Scripture quotations marked NRSV are taken from the New Revised Standard Version Bible, copyright © 1989 National Council of the Churches of Christ in the United States of America. Used by permission. All rights reserved. Scripture quotations marked RSV are taken from the Revised Standard Version of the Bible, copyright © 1946,1952, and 1971 National Council of the Churches of Christ in the United States of America. Used by permission. All rights reserved worldwide. Scripture quotations marked KJV are taken from the King James Version of the Bible. Public domain.

All rights reserved, including the right to reproduce this book or portions thereof in any form whatsoever.

Cover design by: Cornerstone Creative Solutions

For information, address Trilogy Christian Publishing
Rights Department, 2442 Michelle Drive, Tustin, Ca 92780.
Trilogy Christian Publishing/ TBN and colophon are trademarks of Trinity Broadcasting Network.

For information about special discounts for bulk purchases, please contact Trilogy Christian Publishing.

Manufactured in the United States of America

Trilogy Disclaimer: The views and content expressed in this book are those of the author and may not necessarily reflect the views and doctrine of Trilogy Christian Publishing or the Trinity Broadcasting Network.

10 9 8 7 6 5 4 3 2 1

Library of Congress Cataloging-in-Publication Data is available.

ISBN 978-1-68556-254-0 (Print Book)
ISBN 978-1-68556-255-7 (ebook)

DEDICATION

To Sister Anne Marie,

upon whose love and care inspired this fictional story.

Thank you for your willingness to embrace a broken spirit,

nurturing the seed planted so long ago.

For this reason, ever since I heard about your faith in the Lord Jesus and your love for all God's people, I have not stopped giving thanks for you, remembering you in my prayers.

Ephesians 1:15–16 (NIV)

ACKNOWLEDGMENTS

First and foremost, I thank God for His never-ending grace and giving of the Holy Spirit's prodding, which brought this book to life. Much gratitude goes to my loving husband, who listened patiently while my ideas rambled on. I extend many thanks to my family, friends, and countless others who helped guide my transformation. To Mara, who edited the initial manuscript, thank you for your patience and brilliant work. The places in which I reflected, healed, and ultimately grew closer to God are many. I give special recognition to the Jesuit Retreat Center for their hospitality and God-centered programs, which assisted in my faith journey. A note of thanks to the Ignatian Spirituality Institute and Joan for taking a chance on me, sparking a heart on fire for Jesus! To the many retreat facilitators, spiritual directors, and mentors in my life for your guidance, support, and love for Christ. Finally, I honor the memory of Rev. Pat Ferarro, whose homilies spoke to my heart. I pray that Bella's story has given justice to his words, "Turn towards the light, and let the shadows fall behind you."

CONTENTS

Bella's Storm 1
Tears that Sparkle 13
Hidden Blessings 27
A Glowing New Friend 39
A Superhero for God 51
Hungry for Blessings 63
Bella in Lights 75
A Place of Peace 87
Gracie's Song 101
Planting Seeds 111
Where Love Blooms 119
Hide and Seek 133
Friendly Yellow 145
Made to Glow 157
God's Word 169
Beautifully Broken 179
Your Wings Are Ready 191
Let Your Light Shine 201

Endnotes 215

CHAPTER ONE
Bella's Storm

B ella, the caterpillar, led a joyful and inspired life; her personality was vibrant and colored her beautifully. Happy and content with everything, nothing surprised her more than the day her storm blew in. Bella had spent her day among friends and family, admiring the flowers' beauty while running and playing in the park near the tree which she called home. As evening approached, she exchanged hugs, said good night, and headed home.

Thankful to rest all sixteen of her feet, Bella lay down upon a leaf in her favorite tree and closed her eyes. Bella had only been asleep for a brief moment when suddenly the branches on the tree began to move. *There must be a storm coming from the forest*, she thought to herself. Bella had been through enough storms to know it would soon pass, so she repositioned herself to fall back asleep. Having many legs did not make Bella a giant caterpillar; her body was not much bigger than the leaf that she slept on. Even so, she had been able to hold her ground through most storms.

Suddenly, Bella awakened at the sound of a thunderclap and a streak of light in the sky. Fear bubbled up within her, and with each gust of wind, she crouched down closer to the tree. Bella looked up to the sky and thought, *If the rain comes down any harder, I could drown in a puddle on my leaf.* In a flash, it seemed that Bella's entire world was one big storm cloud, and it was taking over all that she knew and loved. As the storm continued, Bella wondered if her friends and family were okay and wished she wasn't in her tree alone. All Bella could do was keep her eyes closed, hold on tight, and wait for the storm to pass.

Occasionally, Bella would quickly open her eyes to check on her surroundings. In one instance, Bella was stunned at the sight of herself.

"Oh, no," she cried out. "My colors have faded, and my stripes are going away. Please help me! Can anyone hear me?"

Bella felt strange. Giving up was not normal behavior for Bella, but this storm was different. If it did not end quickly, Bella feared she would lose everything.

Memories of Bella's life flooded her mind as she lay coiled up in the leaf. A particular memory that kept bubbling up was one of a much younger Bella. She saw herself as a child praying and completely comforted by God. Bella tried her best to recall how to pray and shouted into the wind, "God, you haven't heard from me in a long time, but I need You. Can You save me?"

Hoping God heard her cry, she took in one more deep breath and closed her eyes as tight as possible. At the same time, a big gust of wind forced Bella to snuggle tighter against her leaf. As the thunder clapped and the winds circled, Bella hoped the tree would not let her go. The force of the wind was more than she had ever felt before. All at once, Bella's leaf broke loose, forcing her into the air, through the park, and into the Royal Forest. Panicked and having lost complete control, Bella closed her eyes and cried until the storm and Bella finally came to a stop. At that moment, Bella feared everything she knew about herself was gone.

The storm stripped Bella of not only her colors but also her faith and self-esteem. All that made Bella the vibrant, cheerful caterpillar everyone knew her to be was lost. Eventually, Bella slowly uncurled her body and hesitantly opened her eyes. It was hard for Bella to see because there was a bright light surrounding her. Bella focused her eyes the best she could, but all that she could make out was that nothing was familiar. Exhausted, Bella whispered, "Where am I?"

"You are with me," an unknown voice quickly responded. "I'm down here, underneath you."

Just then, the place where Bella had landed began to slowly move. "Oh, no," exclaimed Bella. "I'm moving again. I don't think I can survive another storm!"

"Relax," replied the voice. "You are okay. You have landed safely with me."

Bella could not imagine what she could have landed on that could be talking to her. Puzzled, Bella rolled over and positioned herself to see what was underneath her. As Bella lowered her face, the fog from the light began to move away, making things much clearer for Bella. Looking back at her were two large eyes, and attached to the eyes was a snail.

The snail giggled at the expression on Bella's face. "Who are you?" Bella asked.

"I am Mira," replied the snail. "You must be Bella."

Instantly, Bella's expression changed from surprise to confusion. "I literally just dropped from the clouds; how could you know who I am?" Bella asked.

"Let's just say a little birdy told me that you would be stopping by," said Mira.

"I don't see how that is possible. I got lost in the storm. It's not like anyone knew I was coming," Bella said.

"There is time for all of that later. Come down from my shell, and let's have a look at you," said Mira.

Bella stretched out her many legs and climbed down off Mira's shell. "I'm afraid I'm not looking very well since the storm," she said.

"Things are looking pretty good from where I'm standing," said Mira.

"You need your eyes checked," said Bella, and she inched closer so that Mira could see her better. "Look at me; I'm all faded and broken. And look at you! Every coil around your shell is so pretty and colorful. Oh, how I wish I could feel as good as you look."

"Settle down, beautiful Bella. You look just as you should, considering everything that has happened," Mira replied.

Bella felt embarrassed by the compliment and quickly changed the subject, "The light is so bright here! Are we in heaven?"

Mira gave Bella a loving smile. "No, my dear, we are not in heaven," she said. "You have landed not only on my back but also on my path. I have much to show you as we journey."

Just then, Bella noticed how comforted she was by the sound of Mira's voice. It provided peace within her. She wondered how she could be suddenly swept away by the presence of Mira, whom she barely knew.

As Bella grew more relaxed, Mira saw this was a good time for some direction. "I have been traveling this route alone for a while, and I could use a companion," she said.

"Are you suggesting I go with you somewhere?" Bella asked.

"Yes," replied Mira. "I am inviting you on a journey," Mira explained that the forest was full of different paths, many of which held adventure and surprise. However, all Bella could see was a single dirt road surrounded by the leaves the storm blew in. On the other hand, Mira seemed to know a lot more about the forest than she did. Fearful of being alone, Bella trusted Mira and agreed to stick with her.

Bella hopped on Mira's shell, and they made their way through the mess the storm had layered upon the path. Bella sat tall to get a bird's eye view of what was up ahead while Mira carried her slowly. They remained quiet, trekking through the debris until they had gotten past the worst of it. Bella spoke up once they came to a clearing.

"I miss my home," she said.

Mira paused. "Stick with me, kid; you are not alone," she said. "Even though this path is unfamiliar, it is full of blessings and surprises."

Bella wondered why Mira would want to do that for her; after all, they had just met. Suddenly, all sorts of questions popped up in Bella's mind, and she could not hold them back any longer. Without restraint, Bella blurted them all out. "Mira, are we going to find a place to stay? Where does this path lead? When will we arrive?"

"You have just been through a traumatic event and have many questions," replied Mira. "Stay close and trust while we travel at a slow and steady pace."

Mira knew there would be time to answer Bella's questions later. The daylight was beginning to fade, and they needed to find a place to sleep. Bella continued to ride on Mira's shell and hoped Mira would not mind one more question. "Hey, Mira," she blurted out. "I was wondering, don't you have somewhere you need to be?"

"Nope," Mira replied. "As I said earlier, I was expecting you."

Mira looked back to see confusion written all over Bella's face. She took some time to explain what she meant. "You see, when the storm came in, I had a feeling that something, or someone, would be coming my way. Then you landed on my shell and looked like you had been through something challenging."

Bella looked away as her eyes welled up with tears at the memory of all she had endured. Mira sensed that Bella did not want her emotions to be so apparent and thought it best to talk about something more light-hearted. "I bet you haven't had anything to eat since before the storm," she said.

Bella thought about it. "I am kind of hungry," she admitted, "but I'm still a little shaken up. It might not be the best time for food."

"Oh, we will not be filling your tummy," replied Mira. "On our travels, your mind and heart will fill with the fruit of the vine. Grace from the Holy Spirit will come upon you in the form of love, joy, peace, kindness, and many other virtues. All of these precious gifts from God will feed your soul."

"I must have landed in a completely different world because I have no idea what you are talking about," Bella said, completely mystified.

"That's okay," Mira replied. "It is not supposed to make sense to you just yet. Hey, that is enough for today, you have been through a lot, and I'm feeling a little sluggish." At a snail's stride, they headed toward a bush on the side of the path. Mira thought it would be a cozy spot to rest for a while.

"Mira, I'm glad I landed on you. I have never been through a storm like this before, and I'm thankful that you caught me and broke my fall," Bella said as they settled in.

"The light sent me to where you would land, and I am glad too," Mira replied. "Sleep now, my little one. Tomorrow is not far away."

"Will you be with me the whole journey?" asked Bella.

Mira snuggled close to Bella. "Of course I will," she said. "God sent me to meet you right where you are."

"You mean the little birdy?" asked Bella.

Mira smiled. "There is enough time for that later," she said. "Close your eyes and think happy thoughts. Tomorrow will be a brighter day."

Mira was content enough to close her eyes and quickly drift off to sleep. However, Bella had so many thoughts racing through her mind that only her body rested. She thought about how beautiful and joyful Mira was and wondered what she would have to do to feel and look that way. She pondered how God sent Mira to find her when He did not hear her cries for His help. For now, the only hope Bella had was in her new friend Mira. Bella closed her eyes. *I better get some sleep*, she thought. *I have a feeling tomorrow is going to be another long day.*

CHAPTER TWO
Tears that Sparkle

Mira was the first to wake up after the much-needed rest and allowed Bella to sleep for a while longer. There was much for Mira to do before they headed out, and she felt it best to make those preparations on her own. Knowing Bella would be looking for her as she awoke, Mira allowed the light to guide her only a short distance away, and in that spot, she prayed.

"Today is a happy day because of You, God! I am grateful to You for the delightful soul that You have placed on my path. I can sense that Bella's wounds are deep and that her faith is fragile. I think I have my work cut out for me, God, but I accept the challenge. I may not completely understand what Bella has gone through, but I trust in You and Your light to guide me as I walk with her towards healing, hope, and transformation."

As Mira continued, the light surrounding her became brighter. "I ask that You have patience with me, and I trust that You will provide me with all the spiritual tools I need. God, thank You for allowing me to help Your child become reborn in Your light and filled with the colors of Your love. Amen."

Upon concluding her prayer, Mira noticed the light surrounding her was now in the shape of a cross. She glanced up to the sky and smiled, as she knew this was God's way of acknowledging her prayer and preparation. Sure that Bella had gotten plenty of rest, Mira returned to where Bella lay.

Mira always moved sluggishly, but this did not stop Bella from hearing her approach. As Bella's eyes met hers,

Mira cheerfully greeted her, "Good morning sunshine, how are you feeling today?"

"I'm certainly glad to know that you are still here," replied Bella.

"Of course I'm still here," said Mira, "I'll always be here for you."

"Well, I wasn't sure if meeting you had been a dream. I'm glad to see that you are real, but I'm also sad that the storm happened too," said Bella.

"I know you are, and that's okay. We will get through this together," replied Mira.

Bella struggled to get the sleep out of her eyes, but when her vision became clear, she noticed something different about Mira. "Hey, your shell has changed," she pointed out. "You look like you are shiny. How did you do that?"

"Look up ahead there. Do you see that light?" Mira asked. Bella followed her gaze and nodded. "When I woke up this morning, I went into the light to prepare for today's journey. Spending time in the light was refreshing, and that shows on my shell."

"Wow, it's like magic! Do you think that can happen to me?" Bella asked.

"In time, my child, your colors will return, and they will be brighter than ever," Mira explained. Bella grew encouraged that she would one day look and feel as refreshed as Mira.

Suddenly, a strange sound very close by startled them both. They soon realized the noise had come from Bella's tummy and burst into laughter.

"It sure sounds like you are hungry! Let's take a nibble so that we have the energy for today's walk," said Mira.

"A nibble might not be enough. Caterpillars are very hungry!" Bella replied.

"Yes, I am aware, but how about we start with just a little nibble at a time? We do not want to be too full for our journey today," replied Mira.

"Okay, you are the teacher, and I am the student. I permit you to lead me. Into the light we go!" shouted Bella.

Once Mira and Bella had fed from a nearby leaf, they headed down the path, walking in the light of the cross set before them. As they walked, Bella began noticing specific things about Mira. Bella particularly loved the different swirly patterns of Mira's shell and delighted in her colors.

Mira had a comforting quality about her, which was good for Bella, as she was missing her old life so very much.

After journeying for what felt like half of the day, Mira noticed that Bella was looking weary. "Hey, let's rest on that log over by the pond," suggested Mira. Bella followed Mira over to the pond and welcomed the rest.

"You've been pretty quiet so far," said Mira. Bella had a lot on her mind and did not hesitate in her response.

"I've been thinking about how lovely you are, and I am lucky to have met you. However," Bella continued, "I cannot help feeling angry and sad about what happened to me. All of these feelings make me want to cry, but I don't want to ruin my time with you."

Mira inched closer to comfort Bella. "Tears are healing. Let them be free from your mind and allow them to fall upon your face. I'll be here to wipe them away."

A special thing happened because all Bella needed was permission to let go. Willingly, she cried and allowed Mira to wipe the tears from her face. As Mira was doing so, Bella noticed a smile upon Mira's face, which baffled her. "What is making you smile?" Bella asked.

"As I wiped the tears from your face, I left a little sparkle," Mira replied. "Let's use the pond as a mirror and tell me what you see."

Eagerly, Bella looked down at the glistening water. "I see a shine on my face!" she exclaimed. "But how can that be, and what does it mean?" she asked.

"That shine is God's light and love," replied Mira. "When you see your reflection, and it's shining, you are seeing God's love within you."

"But isn't God's love always in me, even when my face isn't shining?" Bella asked.

"Yes, and He has given you the shine in your reflection as a visual reminder for you and others to see His love for you," replied Mira.

Having the conversation about God reminded Bella of her concern that God did not hear her during the storm. She thought this would be a good time to ask Mira about it. "Mira," she said, "if God always loves me, even in my distress, how come He didn't hear when I called Him?"

"God did hear you," Mira replied. "He carried you through the storm, where you landed safely with me."

This came as good news to Bella, and her sad feelings were beginning to fade away. However, at the same time, her mind again filled up with questions. "Will the shine go away, or will it stay on my face?" she asked.

"Every time you walk in the light of God's love, you will glow and sparkle," replied Mira.

"Is that why you are so beautiful? Because you always walk in God's light?" Bella asked.

"I have to practice every day, but yes, when I am in God's light, it shows," said Mira.

Bella was starting to connect the dots in her mind, and with growing excitement, she asked, "Okay then, if I practice every day do you think my colors will return?"

"The more time you spend in God's light, the more beautiful you become," replied Mira. Bella's eyes were as big as saucers, and Mira could only imagine what she was considering. "Do you feel better now?"

"I'm a little confused, but I sure do like the way that sparkle looks on my face. Thank you," replied Bella with a smile.

Mira snuggled close to Bella. "It will take some time, but soon everything will make sense, and you will receive what God has intended for you," she said. "Now, I will give you just a little while longer to sit here and be at peace. I will be right here at your side, and when you are feeling ready, we will continue and see what else lies ahead."

After spending a little more time at the pond admiring the beauty around them, Mira and Bella continued on their way. With everything that Bella learned, her head continued to fill up with many questions. Despite her longing to know the answers, she was afraid that the new sparkle might fall off her face if she talked too much. So, fearful of losing her new look, Bella remained silent and waited for Mira to speak first.

"You are quiet over there. How are you doing?" Mira asked.

In a muffled voice, Bella replied, "I'm good," but Mira could not understand the words. Confused and startled, Mira stopped on the path and asked Bella to repeat herself. Again, Bella garbled, "I'm good." This time, Mira looked closely and noticed that Bella was not opening her mouth.

"Why aren't you moving your lips when you speak?" asked Mira. "And please don't respond with a muffle. Open wide, and talk to me."

"I'm afraid if I talk too much and move my face too much, my sparkle will go away," replied Bella sheepishly.

Noticing that Bella looked worried, Mira held back her laughter and said, "Do me a favor, look behind us and tell me what you see."

Bella moved as slowly as she knew how. Once completely turned around, she replied, "I see the light and your snail trail."

"That's right. We are still walking in God's light, so feel free to talk all you want because your sparkle will remain with you," said Mira.

Bella relaxed her mouth and smiled. "I hope you don't think silly of me."

"You are anything but silly, and you have nothing to fret," Mira replied in a gentle voice. "Come on, let's get going. We have more ground to cover before the day is over."

Bella stood as tall as she could, as if she was being instructed by a drill sergeant. "You got it! I'm right behind ya!" she shouted. Bella followed closely behind Mira, making sure to step with all sixteen of her feet into Mira's snail trail. Mira glanced back without Bella noticing and chuckled at this while admiring Bella's determination to maintain her sparkle.

Mira kept to herself, and her mind was calm as they made their way along the path, contrary to Bella's mind, which was filled with all sorts of thoughts and questions. It was almost as if exercise made Bella's brain work harder and at a faster speed. Remembering Mira's promise that her sparkle would not fall off if she talked, Bella sauntered ahead, forcing Mira to stop.

"Hey, there, what's the hurry?" Mira asked.

"I was hoping we could talk again, and I also wondered if you could show me where you live," said Bella.

"You've seen my house," said Mira.

"I have?" Bella asked.

"Yep, you landed on it," answered Mira. Bella stared at her in disbelief. Seeing the confusion on Bella's face, Mira said, "Let's rest on that rock, and I'll explain it to you." Mira had figured she would be the one to talk first, but Bella quickly fired off her questions once they settled on the rock. "Is it heavy? Is it hot? Is it cold inside? Is there only room enough for one? Can I come inside and visit?" Finally, Mira chimed in before Bella could get out another question.

"Why the rush, my dear? You must know that it is customary for a snail to do things slowly and steadily. You listen, and I'll do the talking."

Mira took her time and explained to Bella how her home traveled with her wherever she went. It protected her from danger and most recently broke the fall of someone very special to her. Bella's face lit up with joy, and she was happy with Mira's answers. However, at times, the discussion made her feel sad.

"I wish I could have carried my home with me when the storm hit. Do you think I will ever see it again?" Bella asked.

"I believe that, in time, you will return home. Keep in mind, though, that things will look different there, and you will have changed," said Mira.

"I noticed that your home changes, yet it is always with you. Sometimes when I look at you, I see your colors and sparkle differently," said Bella. Just then, Mira moved as if she were leaving her shell. Bella was stunned. "Wait! What are you doing?"

"I'm simply adjusting to my surroundings, and look, I'm still okay," Mira pointed out.

It did not take Bella long to realize that there was a lesson in this exercise. "Yes, but you never completely leave your home. I have been stripped away from mine," remarked Bella.

"Because that's what snails do," explained Mira. "As a caterpillar, you have different circumstances. God has destined you for incredible things. To achieve them, you will need to learn how to be open to change. This process will become the heart and soul of your new self."

If Mira was trying to get a point across, Bella was completely missing it. "God has a process that will change me?" Bella asked.

"Yes," replied Mira, "and it is already beginning. I see a little color on you." Bella looked down at herself and noticed a small amount of color within her stripes. She recalled what Mira had said about God changing her and wondered if this was the beginning of something new. Perhaps, God had given Mira her colors as well, and if that was so, then Bella had much to look forward to.

Something still did not make sense to Bella, and she felt the need to ask Mira about it. "What about you? Doesn't God have big things in your future?" she asked.

"He led me to you by putting me on your path. *You* are my big thing!" Mira exclaimed.

Bella paused briefly to think about what Mira had just said. "You know something, the best part of that storm is you," said Bella.

Mira gave Bella a warm smile, then glanced towards the sky. "It is good to be you, my dear!" she exclaimed.

CHAPTER THREE
Hidden Blessings

Bella felt good after her heart-to-heart with Mira, and they continued down the path until they were ready for a full night's rest. The next morning, Bella noticed many clouds in the sky, and she wondered if they still walked in God's light even when the sun did not shine. Eager to ask Mira, she gently tapped on her shell to awaken her.

"Hello," Bella whispered. "Mira, are you home?" At the sound of Bella's voice, Mira slowly stretched her head to have a peek.

"Hello there, my little friend. Did you wake up with the birds this morning?" Mira asked.

"No, I didn't hear any birds singing this morning. It's very cloudy today, and I was worried we wouldn't have the light to guide us," said Bella.

"There is no need to be concerned," replied Mira. "I know how to turn the light on when we are ready to go."

"Do you have a magic button inside of your shell to put the light on for us?" Bella asked.

Mira chuckled. "There's no magic button needed. Let us feed our tummies, and then I will show you."

Mira and Bella started down the path looking for delicious leaves and plants that would be a good meal for them. Along the way, Mira explained to Bella how important it was that she first nourished her body before any teaching took place. Mira took her time savoring each little bite while Bella gobbled her food up, leaving only a small piece of the plant to stand on before going to the next. "Oh, boy!" Bella shouted as she slumped down for a rest. Mira giggled at the sight of Bella, who looked like she had grown three times her size.

"Mira," Bella called out. "I think I overate. I hope I have room for the spiritual things you want to feed me today."

"What I will provide you spiritually won't go in your tummy," Mira replied.

"If it doesn't go in my belly, where will it go?" Bella asked.

"As I teach, you will listen closely, and then you will feel it in your heart, and soon it will show in your colors," Mira said.

Bella smiled at the thought. "And in my sparkle!" she shouted.

"Yes. Come on, let's get going. We have Hidden Treasures to find," said Mira.

Bella hopped off her leaf and stayed close to Mira as they went down the path. As they continued, Bella remarked, "I almost forgot. I wanted to ask you a question about the light. Since it is cloudy today, will God's light still find us?"

"Yes, and I'm glad you asked! Now is a good time for us to stop and pray," Mira replied.

"If we pray, does that turn on God's light? I used to pray a long time ago, way before my storm came, but I don't remember the light," said Bella.

"God's light will get brighter and brighter as long as you keep walking in it. There is a shady spot up ahead. Let us rest there and begin," replied Mira.

Mira created a little nest of leaves in the brush not far off the path while Bella waited eagerly for her instruction. "Okay," said Mira. "Let's close our eyes and place ourselves in the presence of God." Bella quickly closed her eyes and, struggling not to peek, kept her ears focused on what Mira would say next. "Hello, God, we thank You for meeting us right here where we are. We are grateful for the meal You provided this morning, for the blessings of yesterday, and those we will receive today. God, we ask You to continue providing your light on our path as we continue on this journey. We know that if the journey gets rough and there are obstacles in our way, You will provide a safe passage. We thank You for bringing us together as new friends and companions on this adventure." At that moment, Bella opened her eyes, and they met Mira's. "Lord," Mira continued, "we ask You to watch over Bella's sparkle each day as she opens her heart to Your love. Amen."

Mira's prayer touched Bella's heart and made her feel loved. Bella kept still, and after a brief moment, Mira broke the silence. "Our prayer has been spoken and kissed up to God. Now it is time for an adventure. Are you ready?"

"I am geared up for anything, as long as it is with you," Bella replied. At once, the sky became sunnier as they made their way back to the path. "Could it be?" wondered Bella, "Did our prayer turn on God's light?" Mira watched Bella as she gazed toward the sky; she knew what Bella was thinking and thought it best to address it.

"Yes, Bella, God has heard our prayer and has put the light on our path," said Mira. "Our job now is to look for His blessings."

The word blessings fascinated Bella; she had heard others speak of them favorably but could not recall any instance of them in her own life. She knew that when others around her received blessings, it made them happy. Bella looked forward to having happy moments and was excited to look for blessings with Mira. Bella kept her eyes to the sky and occasionally looked around to enjoy the beauty this part of the forest had to offer. The path, made entirely of dirt, was wide enough for them to walk side-by-side with some extra wiggle room. Trees and bushes of different sizes lined the trail, some containing flowers and others only leaves. Occasionally, Mira and Bella would encounter a puddle, and each time Bella made it a point to check her reflection. After confirming her sparkle was still there, Bella would smile quickly, making sure not to allow it to fall away. Her bright complexion provided Bella reassurance that God's light remained with them.

    Eventually, they arrived at a crossroads. On one side was a bridge, while on the other, the path continued. Since Mira was guiding the way, Bella did not make any suggestions about which way they should go. She slowed her steps to drop behind Mira and watched her closely. Mira wiggled a little to the left, then to the right before finally approaching the bridge. Excitedly, Mira took a jump out of the dirt and onto the foot of the bridge. Now it was Bella's turn, but she noticed something on the ground just before she took her leap.

    "Look, there is something stuck beneath the dirt," said Bella. Mira quickly turned around to catch a glimpse.

"Yes, there is," Mira replied. "See if you can brush the dust away so we can get a better look."

Bella stepped forward and, with a small swipe of a foot, removed the soil. As she did so, a tiny bit of glitter flew through the air. Thrilled at what she saw, Bella hoped this might be one of God's blessings. "I see glitter and sparkle! What do you think it is?" she asked.

"Perhaps you can get a closer look," replied Mira. Bella lowered herself as close to the ground as she could without disturbing the soil.

"It looks like words. I will remove a little more dirt with my other foot, and then I should be able to see it all," said Bella.

Mira took a step back, allowing Bella to have her moment; after all, she knew God had left this blessing for her. "Okay, I can see it all now. Let me read it to you," said Bella. "The Lord says, 'I will guide you along the best pathway for your life. I will advise you and watch over you.'"[1] Bella read the phrase aloud twice and then, in her quirky way, looked to Mira for an explanation.

"Why are there words on the ground? Are they for us? Is this a blessing?" she asked.

"Steady, little one. God left this to direct you on the way you should go," replied Mira.

Confused, Bella responded, "But I have you to lead me."

"I am here to walk with you. God will be providing the direction," said Mira.

"Well, these words don't exactly tell us which path to take. They are before the bridge, not on it. How do we know to which route God is guiding us?" Bella asked.

"I'm glad you asked," said Mira. "We are going to stop right here and ask Him."

Bella looked all around, up and down, sideways, and backward, but did not see God anywhere. "I don't know how you propose we do that. I can't find Him," said Bella.

"We can go to Him through prayer. We will have a conversation with God and see where He is leading us," said Mira.

Bella thought about this for a moment. "When we prayed the last time, I didn't hear God speak. I only heard you talking. How will I listen to Him now?"

"Conversation with God in prayer takes practice. The more time you spend with God, the easier it will become," replied Mira.

"Have you been talking and praying to God for a long time?" Bella asked.

"I have had a relationship with God all of my life. I knew at an early age that I would dedicate my life to God. I made a promise, and I've been walking in His light ever since," Mira replied.

"You sure are one very special snail. I think *you* are a blessing!" shouted Bella. Mira smiled.

"Thank you," she replied. "Now, let's get to that prayer and see where God would like us to go."

They huddled up close together, relaxing their bodies and lowering their heads, and then Mira began. "Hello, God, we want to say thank You for getting us this far on our journey and for protecting us along the way. We are grateful for the blessing that You have left us, and we come to You now for guidance. We hope to continue walking in Your light and trust You will show us the way."

Mira grew silent. Bella, not sure if Mira was still talking to God, kept her eyes closed. Suddenly, overcome with an urge to offer a prayer of her own, Bella began speaking aloud. "God, I don't know if You have any more blessings waiting for us, but I wanted to thank You for Mira and for helping us to find our way. I am kissing this prayer up to You, and I hope You can grab hold of it." Immediately, Mira glanced over at Bella. They both exchanged a loving smile, glanced up to the sky, and together said, "Amen."

"I feel amazing!" exclaimed Bella. "My heart is fluttering, and it feels happy. I spoke to God! The words just fell out of my mouth!"

"Bella, your prayer was beautiful. You were in the presence of God, and you let Him see and hear the gratefulness in your heart," said Mira.

"Does prayer always make you feel so good?" Bella asked.

"There are many different things which affect prayer, but what matters most is your connection to God. Trusting and believing that God is listening makes those pleasant feelings bubble up inside you," replied Mira.

"Yes, bubbles! Precisely what it felt like inside when my heart was bouncing up and down. It is as if my thoughts were floating around in the bubbles. I let them out of my mouth and up to God's ears. But there's one thing I'm still not sure about. I didn't hear God tell me which way to go," said Bella.

"We asked for God to guide us, and we must trust that He will. God has heard our request. Let's give Him some time to work on it," said Mira.

"Sounds like a plan to me! What shall we do while we wait?" Bella asked.

"All that is required of us is to keep walking in God's light and trust in His timing," replied Mira.

CHAPTER FOUR
A Glowing New Friend

Mira and Bella decided to take a rest, having had a busy morning. They found a cozy spot nestled in the meadow where Mira went into her shell for a nap, and Bella found a leaf on which to relax.

Soon they would make their way back over to the bridge, and with God's help, they would know which way to go.

Bella was the first to awake after the much-needed rest, so she slid from her leaf and headed towards Mira, who was still resting in her shell. Bella knew that there was only room for one but wanted to know what it looked like inside. She climbed atop Mira, rolled to her tummy, and dropped her head down to the opening.

Just then, Mira popped her head out, surprising Bella and forcing her to tumble off Mira's shell. Bella giggled as she landed. "You caught me. I was trying to get a look inside your house. I thought maybe if I stuck my face in before you started to come out, I'd be able to take a look around," said Bella.

"What were you hoping to see?" Mira asked.

Bella thought about this for a moment. "I imagine it's full of God's glitter, light, and all the colors you wear on your shell," she replied.

Mira felt honored that Bella thought highly of her. "What you see of me on the outside is the same on the inside," she said. "There isn't much more to see than that. Now that we have that out of the way, let's get going."

Mira and Bella set out on the path toward the bridge they had come to earlier. Suddenly, they heard a whistle off in the distance. "What was that? And where is it?" Bella asked.

"I'm not sure, but it sounds like it came from just over the bridge," Mira replied.

"It sure is a pretty sound. Can we cross the bridge to locate it?" Bella asked.

"I think that sounds like a good idea," said Mira.

Once Mira and Bella crossed the bridge, the whistle became louder, and they stopped to take a listen. "I don't think I've ever heard a sound more beautiful," said Bella.

"It is extraordinary," said Mira. "I think I will call out to it. Hello, lovely whistle! Where are you coming from?"

"I'm just up ahead," the whistle replied.

Stunned, Bella quickly stuck her feet into the ground and glanced over at Mira. "Did you hear that?" she whispered. "The whistle is alive!"

"I sure did! Let's see if we can find it," Mira replied.

Bella called out, "Oh, whistle, here we are. My friend and I would like to meet you."

Suddenly a tree branch lowered itself right in front of them. Bella peered at the branch and noticed something red upon it. As she bent down to get a closer look, the red dot exclaimed, "Hi there!"

Bella's eyes grew big. "Um, hello, you look like a tiny ladybug. I am Bella, and this is my snail friend Mira. We came this way because we heard a magnificent sound. Was that coming from you?"

"Yes, I apologize. I was singing, and I didn't realize that my voice carried so far," replied the ladybug.

"No worries. We thought the sound was beautiful, and we followed it. We are going on an adventure. Mira is my companion, and we are walking together," said Bella.

"That sounds wonderful! It's been a long time since I've had an adventure," said the ladybug.

Bella turned and whispered into Mira's ear, asking if the ladybug could come along on their journey. Mira gave her a nod of approval, and Bella quickly turned around with an invitation, "How would you like to come along with us? We are walking in God's light and looking for blessings."

"That sounds lovely," the ladybug replied.

"Fantastic, hop off your branch and onto Mira's back," said Bella. "I've landed there before, and it's a pretty good spot to be." The ladybug did what Bella instructed and sat comfortably on top of Mira's shell.

It was then that Bella realized they did not know the ladybug's name, and she asked, "What should we call you?"

"My name is Dottie," said the ladybug.

"Dottie, that name suits you," said Bella. "Let's go and see what other adventures and hidden blessings await."

As they made their way to the path, Bella filled Dottie in on how she and Mira came together. Dottie was fascinated by their story and excited to travel with them. It was a good thing that Dottie was resting while Mira did all the walking because Bella was peppering her with questions along the way.

"Dottie, why were you whistling?" Bella asked.

"I became overcome with the urge to whistle and sing," Dottie replied.

Bella's eyes grew big, and her mouth dropped wide open as she looked at Mira. "The whistle and Dottie, I bet that was God!" Bella shouted. Mira agreed that Dottie's beautiful voice was what attracted them to cross the bridge;

God planned a sound to guide them in the direction He wanted them to go. Bella was excited at this, but something about it bothered her.

How can we know for sure that God sent Dottie as our clue? pondered Bella. Dottie interrupted Bella's thought before she could fully process it. Sitting atop Mira's shell, she yelled down, "Excuse me, look up ahead! There's a light on the path!"

All at once, they looked ahead to where Dottie was pointing, and sure enough, there it was: God's light.

"If you're going to travel with us, you better get used to that light," Bella cheerfully explained to Dottie. "If we pay close attention to Mira and what she teaches us, it will always be there."

Mira stopped so that she could look up at Dottie without tipping her over. Upon doing so, she saw how confused Dottie was. "You are looking at God's light," said Mira. "The light serves as a compass on our journey. We watch for it, and when we see it, we always walk towards it."

"I've heard about that light," said Dottie. "There have been times when I thought I saw it, but I just wasn't sure. I had nobody around me that I could ask."

"You do now," exclaimed Bella. "Mira is an expert on God's light! She's the one who told me all about it."

"You're giving me too much credit," said Mira. "Everything I know is a gift from God, and I am glad to pass the information along to both of you."

"She means it!" Bella said. "We've only been traveling for a short time, and so much has happened."

Bella could feel the excitement building up in her heart and wanted to tell Dottie about everything she and Mira had experienced. Without hesitation, the words poured from Bella's mouth.

"I've learned about the light! I cried healing tears, and then Mira wiped them away." Full of energy, Bella took in a deep breath and quickly opened her mouth again. "You had to see it to believe it when the glitter appeared on my face. Now I sparkle, and it's all because of God."

Dottie quickly started moving around but could not figure out the best way to climb down from Mira's shell. "I need a closer look at the sparkle," she said. Mira gently lowered her head so that Dottie could slide down from the top of her shell and onto the path. Dottie, unsure of what would happen if she got too close, tiptoed slowly towards Bella.

"I have never seen anything like it!" Dottie said. "Bella, you are radiant and beautiful." Bella felt herself blushing. God's goodness towards her had never been so apparent. Dottie skipped closer to Bella, mesmerized by her glow. "What do I need to do to sparkle like you?" she asked.

"It's so easy," replied Bella. "All you have to do is spend time in God's light."

Mira had been quiet during all this time, allowing Bella to shine. However, it was now time for her to step in and aid in the instruction. "Walking in God's light is only part of it," she said. "You also need to allow God into your heart."

"You must not worry," said Bella. "Your face will sparkle in no time if you stick with us."

As they continued to talk, Dottie positioned herself between Bella and Mira, feeling like a ping-pong ball as her head bounced from side to side. Dottie appeared to be losing her patience when Mira moved in, standing face to face with her. "It's essential," Mira said, "to have patience in this process and not get ahead of ourselves."

Bella, feeling left out, wriggled herself between Dottie and Mira. "Slow and steady is the snail way," she explained. Dottie tried to look over Bella's head for Mira's approval, at which Mira gave an approving nod. "Since Mira is our leader," Bella said, "we will go at her tempo."

As they headed out, Mira explained to Dottie how she carried her home with her and that Dottie was welcome to ride along anytime. Bella explained why her colors were so different from Mira's and how God sent Mira to be right where Bella needed her. Dottie was excited to learn these things and enjoyed getting to know her new friends. Prior to arriving in the forest, Dottie was happy in the place where she had lived. After meeting Mira and Bella, she wondered, "Could there be someplace different God wants me to be?"

Bella's tummy was telling her that it had been several hours since their last meal. "Hey guys, I'm getting hungry," she said.

"You are always hungry," Mira laughed.

"I can't help it," said Bella. "That's the caterpillar way. We love to eat and eat."

Dottie found the banter between the two of them comical and chimed in. "I could use a little nibble if you guys want to stop."

"All right," said Mira. "Let's get this hungry caterpillar fed." Mira directed them toward a stream just up ahead.

While they made their way, Bella whispered to Dottie, "When we get close enough to the water, look down at your reflection."

"Why? What if I fall in?" Dottie asked.

"I won't let that happen," Bella replied. "Do you trust me?"

"Yes. I trust you," Dottie whispered with a smile.

As they approached the creek, Bella instructed Dottie to climb up onto her back at the far end of her sixteen feet. "Okay," Bella said. "I have all my feet stuck in the mud. Now take a quick peek at your reflection in the water." Holding on tightly, Dottie looked down.

"My face looks shiny!" she shouted out. "I have sparkle!"

Bella was able to feel Dottie's excitement. "Take a good look, and be careful not to fall off." Bella gave Dottie a few more moments to enjoy her view and then slowly backed herself away from the water so that Dottie could climb down.

"I have sparkle," Dottie said. "But how did it get there? I did not cry like you, nor did Mira touch my face."

At first, Bella thought Dottie had a good point, but she quickly realized how Dottie earned her glow. "You are right," she said. "However, you forgot one other important thing. You have been walking in God's light." Bella surprised herself as she heard her words and realized she was the one teaching Dottie.

All the while, Mira had tucked herself between a few blades of grass and watched the interaction. She was proud of Bella and gave them a little more time at the pond.

"Bella, do we have to move? I don't want the sparkle to fall off," said Dottie.

Bella replied with a chuckle, "Don't you worry about it. Once you've got it, you've got it!"

CHAPTER FIVE
A Superhero for God

Bella and Dottie carefully made their way to where Mira was munching. "Mira, if you have a chance, could you look at Dottie's face?" Bella asked softly.

"There is something spectacular for you to see!" Dottie chimed in.

"I sure hope you two have not gotten into any trouble," replied Mira.

"No," said Bella. "It's nothing like that, but I think it will surprise you."

Mira took one last bite and turned around to see both their faces beaming. She noticed the sparkle on Dottie's face and that Bella's back feet were dripping wet. Not wanting to steal Bella's thunder, Mira asked questions she knew Bella would be excited to answer.

"I must say you both look pretty happy," she said. "What was it you wanted me to see?"

Bella cheerfully replied, "Get closer to Dottie, and tell me if you see anything different." Mira moved towards Dottie to get a closer look.

"It looks to me like someone was playing in the creek," she said.

Bella glanced down and noticed that a puddle had formed under her feet. "Well, I was in the water, but that's not it," she replied. "Look at Dottie's face."

"I have been," Mira replied. "It is such a lovely face. Dottie, you are beautiful."

Bella could not believe that Mira had not yet noticed the sparkle. Quickly becoming frustrated, Bella pointed directly at Dottie's face. "Mira, don't you see? God loves Dottie!" she said.

"God loves everyone," Mira replied. Taking notice of the grumpy look upon Bella's face, Mira decided to let them know she recognized the glitter on Dottie. "Oh, my! Now I see it," Mira exclaimed. "God's love is written all over your face."

"I am so happy to have the sparkle that you both have," said Dottie. "However, I'm wondering how it got there?"

"Yeah," Bella said, "Mira, can you explain that? Could it have come off of your shell when Dottie was riding on top of it?"

"Only God can provide the sparkle. I only help you to see that it's there," Mira replied.

Bella became confused and questioned Mira. "But when you wiped my tears, my glow became alive."

"When I wiped your tears," said Mira, "we were both filled with God's love, and that is where the glow comes from." Bella and Dottie listened intently to Mira as she continued to explain. "Meeting Dottie," she said, "was a blessing on our journey. God's blessings come with love. When Dottie walked in His light, she earned her sparkle."

Bella and Dottie were satisfied with Mira's response, and they decided it was an excellent time to continue down the path. While they walked, Bella shared with Dottie all the things that Mira had taught her since they first met. Mira enjoyed the new confidence coming from Bella and remained half a snail pace behind them, allowing their conversation to grow.

Bella spoke with fearlessness and a joyful spirit. Mira was sure that perhaps one day Bella might be a good companion for others, in God's time. However, Bella had more healing and growing to do before that could happen. Until then, Mira had promised God she would stick by Bella and help guide her to the life awaiting her.

At that point, realizing how far back she was, Mira joined Bella and Dottie as quickly as a snail could move. "Hey, slowpoke," chuckled Bella. "Where have you been?"

"I've been right behind the both of you, getting a good look at God's handiwork," replied Mira.

"God's handiwork?" questioned Bella.

"Yes," Mira replied. "The beautiful friendship growing between you is a gift from God." Dottie and Bella were gleeful at Mira's response and could not wait to find more of God's gifts on their travels.

"What's next on our list for today?" Dottie asked.

"We have much to be thankful for," replied Mira. "It is time for us to take a break and kiss a prayer up to God."

Bella's eyes lit up with joy. "I love it when we pray," she said. Looking over at Dottie, Bella continued, "You're going to like this. I promise." Huddling close, Dottie watched every move Bella made.

Bella lowered her head and closed her eyes, and Dottie did the same. "Relax your body," whispered Bella. "Lean into me while we listen for Mira's voice."

"Hello, God," began Mira. "We wanted to stop and thank You for the beautiful new friend You placed on our path today. We know that You have big things planned for us, and we are ready for all of the blessings coming our way. Thank You for keeping us safe and for loving us."

Mira fell silent, and then as a surprise to them all, Dottie spoke up. "Hello, God, it's me," she said. "Thank You for my new friends and for reminding me that You are here. It has been a long time since we spoke. I feel You have something new waiting for me, and I can't wait to see it." Dottie was quiet now, and her heart was pounding.

Sensing Dottie was through speaking, Mira ended the prayer. "God," she said, "we kiss all of these things up to You. Amen."

"Thank you, Mira. You have done so much for me since I met you," said Bella. "I think it is beautiful how you taught Dottie about prayer."

"I appreciate your sentiment," Mira replied. "God is at work in all of us, and the two of you are great students."

Bella nudged Dottie and instructed her to position her body stout and proud. "Together, we make the perfect God Squad!" she said in a strong voice.

Mira enjoyed the determination on both of their faces. "Okay, God Squad," she replied, "if we want to find more blessings today, we had better get going."

Dottie hopped onto Mira's shell, and Bella followed close behind. In an effort to be just like Mira, Bella mirrored each of her steps, being sure to gather all the glitter from Mira's snail trail that her little legs could hold.

"What are we looking for this time?" Bella asked.

"I don't have a list," Mira replied. "We have to make our way, and we will know when God has sent us a blessing."

Mira's slow speed allowed Dottie to relax, and she thought a lot about the prayer she spoke earlier. *I hope*, pondered Dottie, *the blessing is the answer to my prayer.* Suddenly, Dottie heard a beautiful whistle. "Are you guys hearing what I'm hearing?" she asked.

Mira stopped abruptly to take a listen, causing Bella to bump into her. Mira turned quickly to check on Bella and laughed at the sight of her. Dottie paid no attention to their laughter; she was intently listening for the whistle to happen again. Recognizing that Dottie was trying hard to hear, Bella and Mira quieted down.

Immediately, the whistle sang again. "It sounds similar to Dottie's voice," Bella pointed out. "Where do you think it is?"

"Come together, girls," replied Mira. "We can ask God to guide us to the sound." Suddenly, Bella observed movement up ahead.

"I don't think we need to ask God," she said. "Check out the wiggling bush!" Cautiously, they moved toward the bush for a closer look and a better listen. "It looks to me like the bush is full of berries or flowers," said Bella.

Quickly, Dottie slid down from Mira, crawling into the bush. Once inside, she yelled, "Not flowers or berries; it's a loveliness of ladybugs!"

"Now that you're in," Bella called to her, "ask them what they're doing and why they whistle."

"Okay," said Dottie, and she began speaking. "Hello there! You are all making such beautiful music. May I ask what you're doing here?" One ladybug stepped forward to answer while the rest kept singing at a lower volume.

"We have been here for a couple of days, resting on our journey and waiting for you."

"How could that be?" thought Dottie. "I don't understand," she said.

"We received a message in the breeze telling us to stay in this bush and whistle." Dottie listened eagerly while the ladybug continued, "You see, we are without a spiritual guide. Very recently, we prayed for someone to help us. God breathed your name into the wind, filling the sky with sparkles and light."

As Dottie was gathering information, Bella grew impatient, and she and Mira entered the bush in an effort to see what the fuss was all about. Dottie immediately looked over at Mira, and with tear-filled eyes, she asked, "Could this be the answer to my prayer, my something new?"

Mira, wanting Dottie to answer, responded with a question rather than a solution. "Dottie, how do you feel about asking God if this is the answer to your prayer?"

"I can try," Dottie responded. As Dottie quieted herself, Mira and Bella waited silently. "Hi, God," Dottie began, "Thank You for the beautiful whistling music we just heard and the group of ladybugs waiting for us in the bush. I sure hope You have sent them as the answer to my prayer. You see, God, I miss what it feels like to engage in community. The loveliness You have brought me to is just the right fit and precisely at the right time. If it is Your will, I would like to stay awhile. Amen."

Dottie remained still and silent, waiting for God to respond. Disappointed after not hearing anything, she turned around to join Mira and Bella. The moment she swung around, the ground lit up with light, and the ladybug bush began to glow in every color of the rainbow.

Bella saw this happening and grew excited. "It is the answer to Dottie's prayer," she said. "God has given her a sign."

Dottie fixed her eyes on how beautiful the bush had become. Understanding what this meant, Dottie let her eyes flow with tears of joy. "I have waited so long," she said. "God has given me something new."

Dottie embraced the ladybug, grateful to have met her and the others. She found it hard to contain her joy. "I waited for you for a long time," she said.

"We waited for you too," the ladybug replied.

Dottie motioned Mira and Bella toward her. "It all makes sense now," she told them.

"What makes sense to you, my dear?" asked Mira.

"Meeting you the way I did," responded Dottie. "Beforehand, I was not feeling very confident in my faith or its purpose. Now, having walked with you and Bella, my love of God has a new sparkle."

"The prettiest sparkle I have ever seen," said Bella.

"You're not so bad yourself," replied Dottie. "Perhaps, though, my time with you on this journey changes now. I am needed here to foster the spiritual formation of this miraculous group of ladybugs. God has called me, and my answer is yes." Dottie reached out and hugged Bella. "I will see you again soon, my dear Bella," said Dottie. "You will find what God has waiting for you, I'm sure of it."

Bella held onto Dottie as tightly as possible without squishing her. "I'm happy God answered your prayer," she replied. "These ladybugs are lucky to have you as their gift." Dottie hopped onto Mira's shell and thanked her for guiding her into God's light.

"I hope I can be as helpful to them as you have been to me," said Dottie.

"Enjoy your gift, my friend. We will meet again soon," replied Mira.

Dottie remained with the ladybugs while Mira and Bella made their way back to the path. As they walked along, Bella let out a sigh. "This blessing is a sad one," she said. "I miss Dottie already."

"We must remain positive," said Mira. "Dottie is right where God planned her to be."

"When will I know where God wants me to be?" Bella asked.

"In God's time," replied Mira. "Remember, little one; we must not rush."

"Okay," said Bella. "I trust you, and I believe in God and His timing." No sooner had the words left Bella's mouth than one of her stripes became bright with color. "Hey," shouted Bella. "What is happening?"

"How fantastic!" Mira replied. "Your trust in God is growing, and it shows. God sees it in your heart, but now others can see it too."

Hurriedly, Bella replied, "Let's find more blessings so I can have more color." However, seeing the stern look on Mira's face slowed Bella down as she restated, "On the other hand, let's go slow. I feel like moving snail-like."

CHAPTER SIX
Hungry for Blessings

Mira and Bella found a comfortable place to settle in for the night and reflected on Dottie's happiness and the ladybugs. Bella was confident more good things were yet to come.

As she drifted off to sleep, Bella reviewed some of the things Mira taught her. "God will shine His light on you when you least expect it. To keep encouraged, you have to be patient and believe. Once you learn to give your cares and worries to God, everything will come together." Perhaps the best lesson of the day for Bella was, "Keep going in the direction you're going. God has a path for you to follow, and so far, it's leading you to exciting adventures."

The next day, Mira was the first to awaken. She made her way to the branch where Bella was sleeping peacefully. "Good morning, sleepyhead," said Mira. "Are you about ready to begin?"

Bella leaned forward with excitement and looked down at Mira. "I sure am! I'm ready and hungry as ever!" she said.

"Of course you're hungry," said Mira with a chuckle.

"Hey," Bella interjected, "you didn't ask what I wanted to eat. As it turns out, my tummy is hungry for blessings."

"I can't promise you that we will find blessings today," said Mira. "One thing I do know for sure is that whatever happens, God will be with us."

Bella gazed at Mira with a confident grin and said, "Okay, wise one, but we already have a blessing with us today. We have each other."

"Bella, your faith is becoming beautiful," Mira happily responded. "You're right; today already is a blessed day."

Happy and grateful for one another, Mira and Bella headed onward, seeking God's blessings and nourishment. Mira proposed that they move at a mindful tempo, relishing in the peacefulness provided by the forest. However, this did not stop Bella from munching along their route. It was not long before Bella's tummy grew awkwardly large. "That last leaf was a little too much for my belly to handle," declared Bella.

"I suppose now is as good a time as any to have a rest," replied Mira.

Mira surveyed the area and gestured to a shady location where they could settle in for a bit. Because Bella had not shared her thoughts for much of their stroll, Mira felt it a good time to check in. "So, what do you think of our journey so far?" Mira asked. Sensing a lesson would soon follow, Bella carefully worded her response.

"This part of the forest is precious. I never imagined a forest as tranquil," replied Bella.

At that, Bella closed her lips, hoping that Mira would not probe for deeper feelings on her part. However, Mira, being an effective listener, knew better. "How did you predict the forest would be?" Mira asked.

"A bit like my storm, I suppose. Since the trees are so tall," continued Bella, "I figured the forest would be dark and uninviting. However, it is exactly the opposite."

In the hopes of Bella opening up a little more about the darkness she envisioned in the forest, Mira asked, "What frightens you about darkness?"

"I'm anxious about how I will feel if my world becomes dark once more," Bella responded reluctantly. "I know that God has provided me with blessings since that night, but I can't let go of how horrible I felt in the hopeless moments."

"Sometimes, my dear, change is not all that bad. In fact," said Mira, "if nothing ever changed, there would be no butterflies."

"What do butterflies have to do with change?" asked Bella.

Mira was cautious in her response, as she knew this was not quite the moment for Bella to learn all there was to know about butterflies. "Ever get a good look at a flower before it blooms?" she asked.

"Of course! Usually, the flowers are all closed up," replied Bella.

"Right! What does the flower have to do in order for it to become fully bloomed?" asked Mira.

The answer quickly registered in Bella's brain. "It has to change."

"Exactly," said Mira. "Change is what makes the flowers as special as they were meant to be. The same holds true for you and me, the butterflies, and all of God's creation." At that moment, Mira noticed a tiny bit of sunlight reflecting off the ground. Seeing this as an opportunity for something extraordinary from God and a lesson in reassurance, Mira suggested they move along.

Bella stayed silent while thoughts of upcoming adventures danced upon her heart. She considered that perhaps, her growing relationship with God was part of her life changes. All the while, Bella had not forgotten about the hidden blessings and carefully watched for them along the path. Bella guided her feet with care until a hard object unexpectedly caused her to stop.

At first glance, all Bella could make out was a giant pile of sticks. Hoping this was a hidden blessing, she began to dig through the branches. Mira stood back, watching in anticipation of what Bella might find. Finally, all of the twigs were gone, revealing a stack of what looked like glass rocks tucked into a small hole.

Bella sprang into action, carefully lifting one gem at a time. "How spectacular!" she cheered. "I think we have found buried treasure." Bella's fortune was a mixture of different shapes, colors, and sizes, many of which were so fragile she was afraid to move them. However, something in her gut hinted at the fact that God had left a message in them somewhere. Delicately, Bella removed the pebbles from the ground until only one remained.

Bella reached down to lift the last one, but it was heavier than the rest. It would take all her strength and perhaps that of Mira as well. "If you are not busy over there," shouted Bella, "I could use a little help."

Despite this, Mira remained in the distance. "Now is a good time to exercise your gifts of strength and patience," she said. Bella grumbled at this yet trusted in Mira's expertise.

Digging all sixteen of her feet into the dirt for grip, Bella slowly heaved the stone from the ground. "God," she called out, "strength and patience are a weakness of mine. Please shine Your light upon me." Gradually, the stone lifted, and Bella carefully placed it on the ground next to her. Swiftly, the brightly colored glass turned dark.

"Oh, no," she cried out. "What have I done?" Bella didn't understand what could have happened and considered it her fault that the stone was no longer beautiful. At this time, Mira stepped forward with the reassurance she had been waiting to offer.

"Settle down," Mira urged her. "Take another look at the stone with fresh eyes, my dear."

Without hesitation, Bella wiped the tears from her eyes and looked again at the rock. Bella was startled to see that once again, the rock had transformed and now glowed brightly. Hidden within the shine was a message. Bella grew excited, and she read the passage aloud. "Darkness is fading, and the true light is already shining."[2]

Holding onto the stone, Bella looked toward Mira for guidance. Mira's lessons involved Bella coming to conclusions independently, and for that reason, she did not offer too much insight. However, she did reassure Bella that God would reveal the meaning of His blessings soon enough.

Mira and Bella hoisted the rock upon her shell and moseyed along. All of a sudden, the sky became cloudy, and daylight dimmed. The rapid change in their surroundings shocked Bella, and she needed a moment to be still. "Mira," she called out. "I'm not feeling very well." Mira immediately ushered Bella to a soft patch of grass.

"You look pale," said Mira. "Is it something you ate, perhaps, or is something bothering you?" Bella took in a couple of cleansing breaths before gaining the courage to answer.

"Everything has been so lovely since we started this journey together," she said. "But when darkness comes, it overwhelms me. I wish we had met before my storm and that everything else was the same."

Mira nestled close to Bella to offer comfort. "Change is a large part of everyday life, and God has His reasons for why things happen. Don't forget, God planned for us to meet right when we did," said Mira.

"Will I always be fearful of the dark?" Bella asked.

"You survived a significant loss, the memories of which will remain a small part of you. Sometimes, those recollections will make you feel happy, and other times they'll make you feel sad. However, they make up who you are and what you will become," Mira replied.

At that moment, Bella did not have the urge to respond, so Mira continued. "In this case, dear Bella, the light in your darkness is that God has used change to bring you closer to Him."

Bella grew wide-eyed. "You are right!" she said. "Growing closer to God is good, and He gave me you and Dottie to help that happen."

"He sure did," said Mira. "And there will be others who will help you along the way."

"Oh, I can't wait to meet them!" Bella exclaimed.

"Feeling better now?" Mira asked.

"Yes," Bella replied. "My thoughts are much better, but the clouds haven't gone away. Look, it's still dark. Where do you think God's light has gone?"

"I'm sure there's no need to worry," replied Mira. "Let's get moving. We still have more ground to cover before the day is over."

Bella was not a fan of the clouds and stuck as close to Mira as possible. At one point, Bella followed so closely that she slipped in Mira's snail trail and slid directly underneath her, forcing them both to roll over. Looking at one another covered in snail slime caused them both to laugh. Mira was laughing so hard it knocked her face into her shell.

"Come back out!" shouted Bella. "Let's do that again!" Mira, still laughing uncontrollably, poked her head out of her shell when suddenly, the sky turned black, all except for one glowing cloud not far in the distance.

Not only had the sky changed, but there was also a new warmth in the breeze. Bella was not frightened but was somewhat overcome by a sense of wonder and amazement. "Do you see what I'm seeing?" she whispered.

"I do," replied Mira.

"Do you think God turned that on for us?" Bella asked again with a whisper.

"There is only one way to find out," Mira said.

Bella took off running as fast as she could, moving toward the cloud. She noticed that it swirled and twirled. *That's an odd thing for a cloud to do,* thought Bella, and she ran even faster with growing curiosity. Mira did her best to keep up but could not match Bella's swiftness. Finally, Bella halted directly under the cloud when she discovered a swarm of hundreds and hundreds of fireflies. "Step on it!" Bella shouted to Mira. "This is not your everyday cloud!" Mira scurried toward Bella, and they both followed the fireflies before finally coming to a stop. Just then, the fireflies lit up the sky, revealing a cave entrance.

Bella remained motionless as Mira began to follow the fireflies into the cave. Mira turned back. "Hey, slowpoke," she said. "We had better keep up if we want to be in the light."

With both excitement and fear, Bella trusted that light would overcome the darkness within the depths of the cave. Recalling the message on her rock, she whispered, "Darkness is fading, and the true light is already shining."

CHAPTER SEVEN
Bella in Lights

Drawing near to Mira, Bella whispered to herself, "Close your eyes and be still."

"It's okay," Mira reassured her. "We must trust God and keep our eyes open. We do not want to miss anything He wishes us to see. Hold tight to your stone and when it feels right, look upon it again."

Suddenly, the weight of the stone became much lighter. Quickly, Bella turned it over and looked upon a new message. "God has changed the stone again," she declared.

"What does it say?" asked Mira. Anticipating something extraordinary, Bella read the message. "He who follows me will not walk in darkness."[3]

Instantly, the fireflies adjusted their light, allowing a most striking view. God had used the fireflies to leave messages of light upon all the walls of the cave. "It's a wonderful cave indeed! I see words and phrases, almost too many to count," exclaimed Bella.

"It certainly is," remarked Mira. "Go, little one, inch yourself close and take it all in."

Bella set her stone safely on the floor before making her way further into the cave. The fireflies moved with her, providing light and guidance. "I think I'm close enough now. Yes, I can see!" Bella exclaimed.

"Tell me what you see," said Mira.

"Looks to me like they are all hidden blessings, like what we found on the path," Bella replied. At that moment, Bella noticed a unique sparkle and went to investigate.

"Oh, my," she said. "The fireflies wrote my name in God's light!" Gleeful emotions flooded Bella, and she twirled in celebration.

"Careful not to stir up too much cave dust, my dear," said Mira. "Might I suggest you begin reading the phrases near your name first?"

Bella settled herself, brushed the dust from her legs, and said, "Alright, here I go. This one says, 'Your word is a lamp to my feet and a light to my path.'"[4]

"That's beautiful," said Mira.

"Let me read another," replied Bella. "'Be strong and courageous. Do not be frightened, and do not be dismayed, for the Lord your God is with you wherever you go.'[5] Oh, how fun! Let me try another."

Mira interjected, "Let's stop there for now and reflect on what you read so far."

"There are so many in here we could go on forever," said Bella.

"I'm sure we could, but I think we should just take on a couple at a time," Mira responded.

Bella and Mira found a comfortable place within the cave to sit and chat while the fireflies continued providing

God's light. Mira was the first to get the conversation going. "So tell me, what do you think of all this?" she asked.

"Well, it seems to me the fireflies brought us to a cave of blessings," replied Bella.

"And why do you think that?" Mira asked.

Bella gestured toward the cave walls. "Everybody knows that caves are dark and cold, but this one is beautiful and full of sparkle. It has to be from God," she said.

"What are your feelings about the fireflies?" Mira asked.

"I think God used the fireflies to make sure we would end up here. Like the words about God's light being a lamp to my feet and my path," Bella replied. "The fireflies were like God's pen writing the messages."

Mira loved seeing the excitement within Bella and continued with her questions. "Can you explain to me what you mean by God's pen?" asked Mira.

"I knew for sure it was God when the fireflies wrote my name in the light. I never did tell them what it was, and they certainly did not ask me."

"I can't imagine a better explanation than that," replied Mira. "I think you are spot on, my dear." Mira was excited for Bella and happy that she was aware of the gifts God had given her in this experience. However, she hoped Bella would share more of what was in her heart. "Look around," said Mira. "We are sitting in the middle of God's light and His Word. It is extraordinary and very comforting."

"A fantastic surprise indeed," said Bella. "I couldn't be happier."

To help Bella gain insight regarding her spiritual growth, Mira directed her back to their earlier conversation. "Bella, before we entered the cave, we discussed some of your fears. Having received this grace now, do you feel any differently?" she asked.

Bella considered everything about their day before entering the cave. "God changed our path today by having the fireflies guide us," she replied. "I am learning that not all change results in a bad outcome."

"Exactly," said Mira. "Change will always take place, and there are a couple of important lessons that you should know about how God can help you."

"I am all ears," said Bella.

Mira placed herself in the center of the cave. "There would be no butterflies without change!" she cheerfully shouted.

Bella chuckled at the expression on Mira's face, but she was also perplexed. "There you go again with the butterflies. What kind of change are you talking about?" she asked.

"It's not quite time for that yet, but there are a couple of things you can keep in mind," Mira responded in her teacher's voice.

Bella listened while Mira continued her instruction. "As you go through life, things will regularly change," she said. "Sometimes you will welcome the changes, but other times you may be fearful of them."

"Like my storm," Bella interrupted.

"Yes, your storm is a good example of when to pray for courage," said Mira.

Hmmm, thought Bella, *that reminds me of something.* She turned around to read from the glittered wall.

"Be strong and of good courage,"[6] Bella recited. "Are all of these words from God designed to help me as we go on our journey?" she asked.

"Yes," replied Mira.

"Well then, I have a lot of studying to do," Bella said. "Can I have some time to review more of them before we move on?" she asked.

"Of course," replied Mira. "Take all the time you need, and I'll pray for you in the process."

Bella studied, prayed, and asked Mira questions as she went along. The writings were a lot for her to take in all at once. Bella was grateful for Mira and the fireflies' patience and direction. "Thank you for teaching me so much today," said Bella. "My heart feels all warm and fuzzy."

"You're welcome. The three of us are making a pretty good team," replied Mira.

"Three of us?" questioned Bella. "Oh wait, I know," she continued. "You and me and God!"

Mira's face lit up with a big smile at Bella's understanding. "Let's not forget the fireflies," Mira reminded her. "They carried God's light all the way here." Just then, the fireflies swarmed all around, prompting Mira and Bella to engage in a happy dance in the light of God's Word.

As the day wore on, Bella showed signs of growing in her desire for a closer relationship with God, and her hunger for spiritual food became more robust with each new lesson. She delighted in the ways God was drawing her close, first with Mira, then Dottie, and now by providing light from the fireflies.

Bella was happy to sleep in God's unique cave that night and hoped that as morning returned, perhaps a little color would too. Bella read all that her eyes had the energy to see, then fell asleep surrounded by God's light.

A while later, a flurry of giggles awakened Bella. "Can you keep it quiet over there?" Bella asked. "I am still trying to rest my eyes."

"I can't help it," replied Mira. "Something is tickling me!"

"Oh, all right," said Bella. "Let me come and see what it is." As Bella looked over at Mira, she noticed her shell glowing. "I think I know what is causing you to snicker," said Bella. "Is there any chance that a firefly or two made it into your house?"

Mira was laughing so hard she could not even respond. She poked her head back into her shell, and as she did, a few fireflies made their way out. "Oh, what a relief," said Mira. "I didn't think they were ever going to stop."

"I guess they decided to take a rest with you," said Bella. "I have to say you were looking pretty good with that glow. Maybe you should ask a couple to hang around for a while."

"I am sure God has other plans for them," said Mira. "Since we are wide awake now, perhaps we should be on our way."

Neither Mira nor Bella knew if the morning had come; both the firefly light and the depth of the cave made it difficult to judge. Bella was eager to see what was next on their journey, but she was not sure she had studied enough of God's Word. "I don't know how I'm going to remember everything the fireflies gave me," she said.

"You mustn't worry," replied Mira. "God has written an extraordinary book, one that is a guide for everyone."

"Awesome!" Bella exclaimed. "Where can I get a copy?"

"In time," replied Mira. "Come now, let's be on our way."

As Mira and Bella reached the mouth of the cave, they were not surprised to see that morning had arrived. It was a sunny day, and as they exited, they thanked the fireflies for all their help and hoped to see them again on their journey.

"I think God did something spectacular for us in the cave," said Bella.

"What was spectacular for you?" Mira asked.

"While I was reading the messages," Bella said, "I felt the warmth of the light."

"Can you describe for me what you mean by warmth?" Mira asked.

"Sure," said Bella. "It made me feel like I was at home. I felt loved. God gave me strength as I held onto my rock." Just then, Bella let out a groan. "Oh, no," she cried. "My special rock is still in the cave."

Bella was completely heartbroken, but Mira knew just how to ease her mind. "The Lord is my rock,"[7] she said.

"Did you read that in the cave?" Bella asked, eager for more explanation.

"Yes, and I believe it was a reminder for you that God is always with us. The grace He placed within your rock is now a part of you," said Mira.

Bella's face brightened. "Perhaps God wanted me to leave it behind for someone like me to find," she responded. "I suppose there could be others in the forest in need of the power found within God's light."

"It looks to me like you are learning to put your faith in God," said Mira.

"Is that why I feel the way I do when I'm in God's light?" Bella asked.

"Tell me what that is like to walk in God's light," Mira replied.

Bella wanted to project that she was confident and secure with her words. To do so, she stood as tall as possible, pushing out all her legs as long as they would go. In a powerful voice, she replied, "Since we have been on this journey, there have been days when I struggle with my faith and the ability to give myself entirely to God. Ironically, those become the days when I am blown away by the signs of faith all around me."

Mira paid close attention as Bella continued. "It's almost as if when I get to the point of doubting my faith, I receive God's blessings, which remind me that He is with me and I am not alone."

"Wow, Bella, that was a beautiful reflection," said Mira. "God is capable of more than we can understand. For today, let's focus on following His marching orders as best we can."

At that, Bella stomped her legs up and down. "Where are we headed?" she asked.

"I would like to show you one of my favorite places to relax and enjoy the beauty of the meadow," replied Mira.

"Okay, I would love to see it," Bella responded. "If it's your favorite, it must be beautiful and full of sparkle, just like you!"

CHAPTER EIGHT
A Place of Peace

Bella trusted that Mira taking her to her favorite place was part of God's plan, and she was anxious to see where it was. She wondered if they would find any hidden blessings there. For the most part, their journey had been a flat walk with a few twists and turns. However, the nearer they got to Mira's special place, almost every path became a rolling hill. Bella enjoyed curling up in a ball and sliding down a hill or two, always making sure to wait for Mira upon landing. Each time Bella slid, she dusted off and checked to see how her colors were coming along. Unfortunately, she was unable to see any new changes. Bella slid down one more hill and waited for Mira.

As Mira approached the hill, she saw a concerning look on Bella's face. Quickly, she laid on her back and let gravity take her down to the bottom, almost landing right on top of Bella. "Hey!" Bella shouted. "You almost ran me over, but you did look pretty silly sliding down on your back."

"I was hoping to make you smile," said Mira. "You look sad."

"Oh, you noticed," said Bella. "I've been missing my colors."

"Look on the bright side! You still have your sparkle," Mira lovingly replied. "When it's time, God will completely color you."

"But what does that mean?" Bella asked with concern in her voice. "Before my storm, I had color. I do not feel as sad as I used to, and I am happy learning about my faith. Shouldn't that restore me?"

"Yes, it will, my dear, in God's time," replied Mira. "He knows what you need and when. You must trust in His plan."

"Have you ever lost your color?" Bella asked.

"Long ago, before I had a close relationship with God, if I were sad or hurt, my colors would fade," Mira replied.

"How did you fix it so your color would stay?" Bella asked.

"Once my faith grew, my relationship with God strengthened, and that allowed my colors to stay with me," said Mira.

"You're saying that, once my colors return, if I keep God in my heart and as part of my day, I'll never lose my colors again? Even when I'm sad?" Bella asked.

"You are correct. God does not go around giving colors out willy-nilly. I am very proud of how you pay attention and how eager you are to have God with you," said Mira.

"Oh, I can't wait!" exclaimed Bella.

Now that Bella had things settled in her mind as far as her colors were concerned, they headed out towards Mira's special place. Bella thought about how things might look once they arrived. She pictured many flowers, tall grass, and possibly a pond or two. She checked with Mira for details.

"Are we still going to be in the Royal Forest Meadows?" she asked.

"Yes, we are not leaving the meadow," Mira replied.

"What else can you tell me about this special place of yours?" Bella asked.

"Take a look for yourself; we have arrived!" instructed Mira.

In growing excitement, Bella climbed upon Mira's shell to get a good look.

"How's the view?" asked Mira.

"The trees are as tall as I've ever seen," replied Bella. "I don't see any flowers or a pond. I guess it looks alright, but I was hoping it might be something special."

Sensing disappointment in Bella's voice, Mira quickly responded. "This place holds special meaning for everyone individually. We will spend some time here, and God will reveal to you its meaning in your life."

"How did God make it meaningful for you?" Bella asked.

"Let's walk a little while," replied Mira. "I'll share with you my story and the blessings I received, which dwell deep within my heart."

Mira knew how important it was that she share these details with Bella in the hopes that Bella would one day do the same for others. Soon, they happened upon a clearing on the path with trees on either side that provided an arch above them. "Look up," said Mira. Bella did as Mira asked, and as soon as her gaze fell upon the arched trees, they parted in a most inviting way to reveal God's light.

"Wow!" exclaimed Bella. "It's like the trees and God are welcoming us."

"Yep! That is what it felt like the very first day I arrived," said Mira. "You see, I was not acting in a very brave way that day. Unaware of what I would experience and what my time would be like spent in this place, I arrived with fears."

"I cannot imagine you being fearful," said Bella.

"I have fears and concerns the same as you do. I've just grown in the way I address them by bringing God into those moments. Anyway, when the trees opened, and I saw God's light through them, I knew something special would take place."

Mira's shell suddenly brightened as she recalled that most precious moment. Bella took notice and held onto hope that this place would do wonders for her as well.

Carrying joy in their hearts, Mira and Bella moved through the welcoming arch. Their conversations were such that neither realized how much of the day had passed. Mira would talk as Bella fired off her questions. Finally, Bella became quiet, and Mira realized the daylight had begun to fade. Finding a comfortable place to rest for the night, both Bella and Mira snuggled in.

Thankful for everything the day brought, they kissed a prayer of gratitude up to God. Before drifting off to sleep, Bella asked, "Are we staying here for a while?"

"We will hang around here as long as God needs us," replied Mira. "I have a feeling there is something special for you to do here."

"Now you have me excited, and I don't know if I'll be able to sleep!" Bella exclaimed.

"Try counting your blessings," said Mira.

"I don't know where to start," Bella replied.

"Start by thinking about all of the gifts God has given you on this journey, and tomorrow you can share them with me," said Mira.

"Sounds good to me! Good night, my good friend," said Bella.

"Good night, my little one," said Mira. Bella closed her eyes and quietly began to recall her blessings, one by one, and before long, she fell asleep.

The light of the next day came quickly, and Bella gave her body a big morning stretch. Feeling refreshed and rested, she climbed down from where she slumbered. Bella was sure Mira was in prayer and wanted to begin that same routine. *Why not start right now?* she thought. *I'll need a sunny and quiet place.* Just then, she spotted a flower garden. The flowers were colorful, and the lush greens provided a comfortable place to be still. Bella closed her eyes, quieted herself, and began a prayer.

"Hi, God, it's me," she said. "I want to do this with You every day, and I am asking that You please remind me when I forget." Hesitating briefly, she thought about what should come next. "Oh! Gratitude!" she exclaimed. "Thank You for the blessings that I counted last night, especially for Mira. She is the biggest blessing I have ever gotten. I know that You sent her to me. God, I love You for that, and I love Mira very much." Just then, Bella paused, not knowing what to say next. "God, I know I'm not the best at prayer," she said, "but please give me some time, and I will be better at it one day. Amen."

Reveling in her prayerful moment, Bella remained in the flowers, enjoying the colors and fragrances surrounding her. She noticed that one flower stood brighter and more significant than the rest. *I bet that flower smells amazing*, Bella thought. Sticking her nose in the center, she took in a deep breath and enjoyed the perfume. Bella took pleasure in the softness of the petals and knew this was a blessing from God.

As she embraced her time in the flower, Bella grew excited to tell Mira about her experience and count it as a blessing later. Wanting one more whiff, Bella bent lower to smell the fragrance. However, as she lifted her head out, her ears detected an odd chirping sound. Bella quickly surveyed her surroundings, but it was not clear where the noise was coming from. *Perhaps*, she thought, *I have been on this flower so long that my legs are sticking*. Dismissing the noise as her own, Bella sprung from the flower to see what was taking Mira so long.

As Bella's legs reached the grass, she heard the chirp again, but this time it was louder. It became clear to Bella that she was not the noisemaker. *There must be someone else nearby,* she thought. Slowly, she began to move through the garden. "Hello," Bella faintly called out. "Is someone there?"

Just then, Bella could see blades of grass moving right in front of her. Fearful it was something much bigger than herself, Bella scooted a half step away and called out again. "Hello! Mira, are you hiding in the grass?" Suddenly, the blades of grass started to part, and out hopped a grasshopper.

"Whoa," said Bella, "Who are you?"

The grasshopper sprung towards Bella and replied, "I am Gracie. Who are you?"

"Hi, Gracie, I am Bella," she replied.

"I'm glad to meet you," said Gracie. "What brings you to my garden?"

"All of this is your garden?" Bella asked.

"Well, it's not all mine, but it is my home. I like to call it my place of peace," replied Gracie.

Bella's eyes opened wide. "That is what my friend Mira calls it, too!" she said.

"Oh, you are Mira's companion!" Gracie replied.

"Hey, how do you know that?" Bella asked.

"I bounced into Mira this morning," replied Gracie. "She was praying by the pond and told me all about you."

"Do you know where she is now?" questioned Bella.

"Mira wanted to spend the day with God, and she has asked me to be your guide for a little while," Gracie reassured her. "She will catch up with us later."

"I don't know about that," replied Bella. "We were supposed to talk about the blessings I counted last night. She must have forgotten."

"I am sure that's not the case," said Gracie. "Let's take a walk, and you can tell me all about your blessings."

"Okay, but let's not wander too far," said Bella. "I don't want Mira to think I have gotten lost."

"Don't you worry, little one, Mira knows just where to find us," said Gracie. "You are safe with me."

Bella gasped when Gracie called her little one. Mira was the only one who addressed her in that way. Needing an explanation, Bella asked, "Why did you call me little one?"

"Mira spoke highly of you, even though you are small in stature. She referred to you as her little gift," replied

Gracie. "I thought it was fitting since God has brought me to your side."

Bella was confused. "God brought me to your side?" she asked.

"Yes, God placed me on your path this morning," said Gracie. "He provided the perfume in the flower as a way to keep you still, giving me a chance to find you and make myself known."

"I stopped to smell the flower, and I was able to hear you in the grass," Bella responded with excitement.

"That's right," Gracie said. "If you had kept walking, you might not have listened to my call."

A big smile appeared on Bella's face as she personally acknowledged Gracie's sound as a call from God. *Just like when God gave Dottie the whistle*, thought Bella.

Gracie, enjoying the expression on Bella's face, knew that Bella was receiving insight from God. Wanting to keep that motivation going, Gracie led Bella out of the flower garden to another area where she hoped Bella would be inspired to share what was in her heart.

"Here we are," said Gracie as she hurdled forward. Bella paused to look around, and the only thing she could see was a very tiny hole cut into a huge rock. Noticing that Gracie was still skipping ahead, Bella hurried to catch up with her.

"Wait for me," she said. "I don't want to go in there alone." Gracie turned to give Bella a reassuring glance and motioned for her to follow. Once inside, Bella's mind was happy and energetic, and she suddenly had questions. "Where are we? Why is this rock hollow? What is it called?" she rambled.

"It doesn't have a name, but to me, it feels like peace and serenity," Gracie replied.

"How can a rock make you feel like that?" Bella asked.

"It depends on how you use the space," replied Gracie.

"I don't know what you mean," responded Bella. "All I see here is darkness with a spot of light where we entered. What can we possibly do in here?" Bella asked.

"In time, how you see this place will change," replied Gracie. "When I first found myself here, it was dark, just like it is for you. Now, as I look around, I see the light and happiness."

Bella closed her eyes tight, then opened them quickly and looked around. "I think you see things a lot differently than I do," she said.

"It's okay," said Gracie. "Together with God, I will help you see the beauty. You cannot see it now, but there is probably a message here somewhere."

"Well, it better be a good one," snickered Bella. "Actually, now that I think about it, this looks similar to my cave of blessings. It was the most God-kissed place I've ever seen."

"How lovely that sounds," said Gracie. "Here, sit here for a bit, and you can tell me all about it." Bella was inspired to share how God led them to the cave and wrote her name in glitter. Gracie's listening presence provided much comfort to Bella, giving her the freedom to tell Gracie everything.

CHAPTER NINE
Gracie's Song

Nestled together in a cozy corner, Bella shared the circumstances of her life before the storm and the events that took place as the storm blew in. It was painful for Bella to recall that day. However, it also was a way for Gracie to understand Bella's heart. While Bella was revealing all that had happened, tears welled up in her eyes.

"What is it?" Gracie asked.

"Remembering everything about my storm always makes me sad. But now, sitting here with you, I feel warm and even happy," Bella said.

"A good way to process what you are feeling," Gracie said, "is to focus on what you have gained. Where did you say you landed when the storm ended?"

It only took Bella a split second to respond. "I landed on Mira!" she exclaimed. "I gained Mira! Oh, what else is there? I gained the cave of blessings, as well as Dottie and her new family. Then there was God's Word on the path, the red rose, and you!"

"You have gained a lot and have much to be thankful for," said Gracie. "It is okay to have a longing for your past mixed in with the happiness of your present moments. God's love shines through the darkness, and that is why you can find happiness in despair."

Suddenly, Bella's eyes welled up with tears again, and she lowered her head in disappointment; she had left out an essential blessing. Pretty sure of why Bella was feeling this way, Gracie snuggled up against her. They were quiet until

Bella spoke up. "Gracie," she called out, "I feel horrible about something."

"It's okay, my child; God understands," Gracie replied. "Mira told me about your journey and how you have grown in your faith. I have seen the excitement in your eyes, and you glow when you talk about your new relationship with God. So, when you listed all of your blessings but didn't give credit or acknowledge God, I knew this would affect you."

"How could I forget God?" Bella asked.

"It's not that you forgot Him, Bella. Gratitude is part of your faith that requires practice. God knows this, and He is patient in your learning," Gracie continued. "God's work in us is fantastic, and one day when you are sharing your story, you won't even hesitate to offer gratitude to God first."

A befuddled look came upon Bella's face, as she could not imagine being as upfront with others as she had with her new friends. In response to this look, Gracie said, "The good Lord has plans for you. Someday, He will use you to lead others to Him."

"Like how Mira is leading me?" asked Bella.

"Exactly," replied Gracie.

"I'm afraid I don't know much about leading others towards God's light," Bella said with no trace of confidence in her voice.

"Give it time," Gracie replied. "You are an eager student, and Mira is a great instructor. Speaking of which, I bet she is ready for us. Why don't we go find her?" Bella nodded.

As they exited the rock, Mira had placed herself in a noticeable portion of the path, allowing her to see Bella and Gracie approach. "I see some happy faces!" she cheered.

"Yep!" responded Bella. "Today was a perfect day!"

"I can't wait to hear all about it," said Mira.

"Not so fast," Bella replied, "We gotta eat. Being peaceful and happy has worked up an appetite!"

Having mutually agreed, the three of them wandered off looking for yummy plants to fill their bellies. Bella, in-between mouthfuls, let Mira in on all that Gracie had taught her. Suddenly, though, her tummy grew full, and a desire for some alone time bubbled up. "You both deserve a pleasant visit," she said. "I think I'll go for a little hike."

"Be sure not to go off too far," responded Mira. "Meet us back at the hollow rock just before sundown." Bella happily agreed to the terms Mira laid out and began to wander through the grass.

There were so many thoughts running through Bella's mind, and she needed some quiet time to process everything. Bella continued moving about, hoping to find the right place to rest and reflect. As this area was new to Bella, she did not wander too far. She could hear the sound of trickling water off in the distance and headed in that direction. Many things in nature brought comfort to Bella, but perhaps the one she adored the most was the soft, slow dribble of a waterfall.

Finally, her eyes gazed upon the most spectacular of all waterfalls. *Oh, how beautiful, and just what I needed*, Bella thought. She looked up to the sky to thank God for guiding her to this spot. *There's so much I want to say and consider. I don't know if I should pray or keep it all in my head. Okay, let's not get frustrated or upset. Think Bella! What would Mira and Gracie do?*

Immediately, she closed her eyes and inhaled a giant breath. As Bella released the breath, she could feel her body become loose and free. All sixteen of her legs relaxed, and Bella was comfortable. *That's it*, she thought. *Sit and be still. Allow yourself to be still in the presence of God. I do not need to tell God I am here. He will find me and meet me where I am.*

Bella continued to organize the thoughts in her mind, lifting them to God as if she were talking to a friend. Her conversation was not formal; she did not begin or end as if it were a prayer. "There is something about the sights and sounds of water that feels as though You are calling me toward You. Even with my eyes closed, I am at peace and comforted, knowing You are its creator."

As she lifted these thoughts and words toward God, she began feeling as if He were holding her near. Imagining a hug from God encouraged Bella to continue. "I have many new friends, God. Oh, how exciting it is to consider You a friend too! I think that is exactly what I need!" Knowing that the best of friends tell each other everything, Bella spilled her thoughts one by one.

Feeling confident she had accomplished what she set out to do, Bella brought herself back to the present moment. As she took one last look at the waterfall, she noticed the sun beginning to set. Somewhat fearful of being alone in the dark, Bella hastily made her way back to the hollow rock. As she rounded the bend, Bella heard what sounded like violin music. She hurried her steps, excited to discover where it was coming from. Approaching the rock, she noticed a glow coming from inside. Bella yelled out to see if Mira and Gracie were nearby, but there was no response. Hoping that they were already deep within the rock, Bella entered.

Bella was quiet, and as she made her way through the hollow walls, she noticed the rock had changed since earlier that day. The darkness had gone, and instead, she saw a golden glow. Moving with caution, she kept her eyes wide open, enabling her to see clearly. Soon, Bella noticed Mira resting on a pebble. "There you are," she said. "I was beginning to wonder if I had entered the wrong rock."

"Hi there," Mira replied. "Have a seat and join me." Bella peered forward as she took a seat and then realized the music she'd heard was coming from Gracie. Bella had never seen or heard anything like it. All around Gracie was the golden glow, and she was moving her leg against her wing to create violin sounds.

The music was peaceful and began to touch something within Bella. As she listened, she gazed at Mira from time to time, and in her, she saw serenity. As Gracie moved with the music, Bella saw a harmonious trait. *Perhaps a gift from God,* she pondered. All the while, Bella began to understand why this place was so special to Mira and Gracie.

Bella allowed her peaceful thoughts to settle; she noticed Mira leaving and positioned herself to follow. As soon as she saw Bella behind her, Mira whispered, "The music is for you. Stay here and delight in it for a while."

"No, wait," Bella replied. "Please share this with me."

"I have some things I need to take care of before beginning the rest of our journey tomorrow," Mira said. "You stay here and let Gracie keep you company. God has given her this most beautiful gift, and she wants to share it with you."

After they said goodnight, Bella relaxed and continued to admire Gracie's music. It was not long before Bella felt something special happening inside her. As the music continued to play, the golden glow deepened, and so did the feelings in Bella's heart. At this moment, Bella lowered her head and felt as though God was speaking to her. She let herself accept the way her body was feeling, and soon tears graced her cheeks. *Tears are healing,* she recalled, and she embraced each one that fell. There was something different about her tears this time, though; they were bringing her joy.

Gracie noticed outward changes occurring in Bella as the sparkle on her face had brightened from a distance. Sensing that this was enough for one day, Gracie softened the music a little at a time and then went over to sit with Bella. Not wanting to startle her, Gracie waited a few moments before making herself known. Bella, deeply relaxed, did not notice the music had stopped until Gracie gently leaned against her side.

"Oh! Hi there," Bella said.

"I'm sorry, I didn't want to interrupt you," Gracie replied. "Have you enjoyed yourself tonight?" she asked.

"Yes, very much so," Bella replied. "You have a beautiful talent. Your music was very inspiring and helpful. I can't thank you enough."

"I'm glad the music was pleasing for you," said Gracie. "Is there something in particular that stood out for you as I was playing?"

"The music made me feel safe and secure in a way that feels like a blessing," Bella said. "As I listened to every note, I could feel God making me stronger."

"That's wonderful," Gracie commented. "It sounds to me like you shared some extraordinary moments with God tonight."

"I feel like something remarkable has happened," Bella replied.

"What is that?" Gracie asked.

"I believe the pain in my tears has turned to joy and love," said Bella.

"Can you tell me why you feel that way?" Gracie asked.

"God has made me feel that way," said Bella. "It's in my memories and the way I see them in this place. When I look at them now with God in my heart, I can see that He was there with me. God has cradled my pain in His love."

"That's pretty amazing," said Gracie. "Is there anything else you would like to share?" she asked.

"Yes!" Bella exclaimed. "God has blessed me with my experiences and placed friends into my life that would not be there if the storm had not come. I am blessed to be where I am right now, and it is because of my storm. I thank God for that."

"Bella, you have been a wonderful gift to both Mira and me, and for that, we thank God," said Gracie. "Rest now, my little one. Tomorrow will be upon us soon."

CHAPTER TEN
Planting Seeds

That night in the hollow rock, Bella and Gracie slept peacefully. At the same time, Mira prepared for what was next on their journey. Prayer was the groundwork needed as a means to confirm God's call. Mira had not forgotten how grateful she was for Gracie's assistance in helping Bella open her heart and hear God's voice, and she extended her thankfulness to God.

Gracie awoke early the following day, and she met up with Mira for prayer. "Good morning, friend! Your little one is still resting comfortably," she said.

"How did it go last night?" Mira asked.

"The evening went splendidly," replied Gracie. "Bella was very aware of God's presence."

"Oh, happy day!" exclaimed Mira. "I cannot thank you enough for accepting God's request to use your gifts and inspire Bella."

"Spending time with Bella and watching her blossom was a gift in itself," said Gracie.

"Mira, you have lit up that girl's world. She is reacting to your pace, and you have governed her steps."

"That is sweet of you to say," said Mira. "However, Bella is walking in the steps that God has laid out. I am simply the instrument moving her along."

In agreement, they offered a loving glance to God; in doing so, Mira noticed the sky was a different shade of blue. "Perhaps there is a storm rolling in," she said. "We had better get to Bella. The sky does not look very happy this morning." At that, Gracie hopped over Mira's shell, getting a head start.

As they approached the rock, Bella heard Gracie hopping around, and when she opened her eyes, Gracie and Mira looked upon her with great big smiles. "Well, you two look like you have been up to something. What is up?" Bella asked.

"We are excited for the day," Gracie replied cheerfully.

Bella quickly noticed the sound of rain as the storm suddenly arrived, echoing loudly through the rock. While fear quickly filled Bella's mind, Mira suddenly headed for the rock's opening as fast as a snail could move.

"Wait! What about the storm?" Bella called out to her. Bella rushed to Gracie, huddling close to her side, and the two of them hurried after Mira. As they approached the opening, the rain's sound grew louder and louder, making Bella frightened. "Mira, where are you?" she cried out.

"Not to fret, little one," Mira called out. "I am over here." Bella and Gracie followed the sound of Mira's voice, exiting the rock and quickly getting soaked by the falling rain.

In an instant, their eyes beheld quite the sight. Mira had positioned herself perfectly under the tallest mushroom they had ever seen. "Check this out!" urged Mira. "God has given us an umbrella. Come on over and join me." Bella and Gracie hurried to the mushroom, where they all gathered in one big clump.

Bella was still looking up to the sky. "Might a big storm take me away again?" she wondered. "Hold on tight; I think the wind is picking up," she said.

"I would not worry about it," said Mira. "I see friendly raindrops."

"How can you tell they are friendly?" Bella asked.

Mira smiled. "Because they are glowing!" she sang out.

Bella leaned out from under the mushroom for a peak. "Oh, boy!" she cheered as she ran out into them. "They are glowing! Gracie, do you see this?" Bella asked.

"Yes, and I can see you dancing in them," Gracie replied. Mira and Gracie were gleeful as they watched Bella spinning around, playing, and dancing among the sparkling rain.

Bella spun herself around like a helicopter, twirling and embracing the feeling of the water dripping upon her. "Did God make the rain glow?" she yelled out.

"It looks that way," Mira replied. "God saved your healing tears for the perfect time. Now, God is raining them down on us to bring joy and new hope for the remainder of our journey."

Bella, filled with excitement, shouted out, "God, thank You for this rain! With guidance, You and I dance."

As Bella continued to spin around and dance in the rain, Gracie noticed the ground becoming soft, leaving holes where Bella's feet had been. Gracie turned to Mira. "Now is the time," she said softly.

"I think you're right," said Mira, who also noticed Bella's footprints. Mira and Gracie blew a kiss up to God. At that moment, the clouds parted, and the rain stopped. It took Bella a few moments to realize that the rain had gone. It was not until the sun shone brightly into her eyes that Bella stopped in her tracks.

"Bella, don't move," said Mira.

"I can't move. The mud is holding my feet," Bella said with a grin.

Mira replied, "God has given you a gift, and we need to figure out how to use it."

"A gift? What gift?" Bella asked.

In response, Mira held out a handful of seeds. Bella tried to get a closer look at the seeds, but her feet were deep in the mud. She peered at Gracie, hoping that she knew what Mira meant. Gracie worked to free Bella from the mud, tugging her feet out one at a time, then sat her down to explain God's work and the gifts Mira had spoken about.

"What is Mira holding in her hand?" Bella asked.

"Those are seeds," replied Gracie. "Seeds of faith, hope, and love. They blew in with the rain, and we are going to plant them in the holes you've made."

"That sounds like work," said Bella. "When does the gift arrive?"

"Our gift is already here," explained Gracie. "It's in the act of planting each seed. Those who feed on the plants will receive gifts in their heart."

"How can planting a seed be a gift?" questioned Bella.

"Pay attention to how you feel as we go along. In time you will notice changes happening in your heart. Those changes are a gift from God," replied Gracie. Bella, eager as ever to receive God's gift, hurried to Mira.

"Let's go! I'm ready to do God's work," said Bella.

"Alright then," Mira replied. "Off we go!"

Mira led them as they went along, and Bella studied everything Mira was doing. Mira placed each seed into a hole and moved to the next with care. Bella's job was to cover each seed with fresh soil. Gracie stayed well behind and prayed over each planted seed.

Bella was happy she was doing God's work, yet she questioned the reasons for this exercise. "Hey, Mira," she called out. "How long does it take these seeds to grow? What will the plants look like? Will there be flowers on them? Will they smell pretty?" Bella opened her mouth to continue spilling out her thoughts, but Mira interrupted.

"Bella, you ask great questions," she said, "but let's slow things down and make sure we are not interfering with planting."

"Okay, I'll work at your pace," said Bella. "Even so, I want to understand the purpose of putting them in the ground. I thought faith, hope, and love come from the heart."

"That is right," Mira responded. "But these virtues also need to be nurtured to grow. Not everyone has them in their heart, and these plants can provide a little bit of help."

Just then, Gracie put in her two cents on the matter. "Once the plants grow, they become food," she said. "Food that is full of God's goodness."

"Like the spiritual food that Mira has been feeding me?" Bella asked.

"Exactly," replied Gracie. "Mira has been doing an excellent job of providing you with spiritual food for the journey. Sometimes though, Mira and I cannot be with our companions, so God has given us another way to provide spiritual fruit by allowing us to plant the seeds."

"Wow! Super cool," said Bella.

"The answer to your questions is that these plants become what God intends them to be," continued Gracie. "He has a plan for them and knows who needs to feed upon them. Our job is to plant the seeds."

"Oh, so it's like how God knew that I needed to land on Mira so that she could give me spiritual food," said Bella.

"That is precisely it, Bella," Gracie said. "I have an idea. Let's finish up here, and I will show you what they look like in full bloom." With that, they all went back to God's work. The sun was shining, birds were singing, and the three of them were renewed and refreshed in God's light.

CHAPTER ELEVEN
Where Love Blooms

Happy emotions filled Bella's spirit as she covered the last hole and quickly turned to watch Gracie pray over it. Bella recognized how beautiful Gracie looked in God's light and admired Mira's glowing shell further up ahead of them. Once Gracie had concluded the final prayer, she and Bella met up with Mira.

"How many seeds do you think we planted today?" Bella asked.

"I didn't keep count, but that does not matter to God," replied Mira. "It only takes one to produce a lot of fruit."

A scowl suddenly came over Bella's face. "One seed!" she exclaimed. "I spent the entire day patting and carefully placing dirt over a lot more than one seed!"

"Not to worry, Bella. God has a plan for all of the seeds you helped us to plant today," Mira reassured her. "Each one has a purpose, and it brings joy to God and us knowing that you were a part of it."

"It sure was a tiring job, but I am glad I was part of it, too," said Bella. "Thank you both for teaching me and for showing me how to plant God's seeds."

"You did a fantastic job, Bella, and you are glowing even more in God's light," said Mira. Bella quickly looked around for the closest puddle to see her reflection. Sure enough, another one of her stripes was full of sparkle and color.

Bella held back tears. "Thank You," she whispered up to God. "Have we been walking in God's light all day?" she asked Mira, as she had been too busy planting seeds to notice.

"Yes, and God will continue to guide us on our way," Mira replied.

"Okay, then where to next?" Bella asked, looking around to see where the light was shining.

"Follow me," answered Gracie. "I will show you what God's fruit looks like when the seeds bloom."

They had not traveled too far up the path before Bella noticed a tree off in the distance that was so bright it looked like it was on fire. As they got a little bit closer, she saw it was wiggling. "Whoa, what is in that tree?" she asked.

"That tree was once a seed and has bloomed where it was planted," replied Gracie.

"You mean that it's God's fruit?" Bella asked.

"Not quite," replied Gracie. "The seeds produce the plant, and when God sends His children to feed on it, the fruit within its branches becomes part of their heart. That is where faith, hope, and love bloom."

"Well, I have never seen so much light in a tree before," said Bella. "It is breathtaking, but what makes it wiggle?" she asked.

"Scurry a little closer and take a look inside," Gracie replied.

Bella moved cautiously toward the tree. The trunk contained many different-sized holes, each encircled by an orange glow. Choosing the hole that fit her best, Bella entered the tree. She felt both anxious and excited about what she might find, all the while hoping that whatever was eating from the plant was not very large. Gracie and Mira allowed Bella to explore independently, giving her time to become familiar with her surroundings while also granting themselves a quiet rest.

Bella had tiptoed for a few moments when she heard a loud crunch, making her stop suddenly. Feeling fearful, she closed her eyes for just a moment and quietly asked God to protect her. "God, I know I'm walking in Your light, but I can't help feeling a little scared right now," she said. "Please don't let whatever is in this tree eat me." Just then, Bella heard laughter. She opened her eyes, and looking back at her was a fat, glowing caterpillar with leaves hanging from his mouth.

"Hi, I will admit that I am always hungry and can eat all day," he said, "but you do not look very appetizing to me."

"I am sorry, I heard you and became frightened," said Bella. "My friends sent me in here and didn't tell me what I would find."

"I hope you are not disappointed," said the caterpillar. Bella loved making new friends and welcomed his presence.

"Not at all!" she said. "I am Bella. It's nice to meet you."

"Hi, Bella, I am Andy. By the way, I loved your prayer," he said.

"Thanks, I am learning to go to God when I am afraid," Bella replied.

"I didn't mean to scare you," said Andy. "I heard your voice, and it sounded sweet and new. I had to check it out."

Bella stepped back to get a good look at her new friend and noted his plump appearance. "You look well-fed. Have you been here long?" she asked.

Andy glanced down at his large tummy. "Yes, I've been here a while," he said with a wiggle, "but it's not just me. There are many others here. I'll introduce you to the gang."

As Andy led Bella through the tree, she walked closely at his side, taking in all she could see. Around her, she could hear the sounds of munching, crunching, buzzing, and fluttering. "Where are all the noises coming from?" Bella asked.

"Just the gang," replied Andy. "You can hear all those who are feeding on the spiritual plant."

"There must be a lot of them," said Bella.

"I'd say there is a fair amount," Andy replied. "Lucky for us, they gather in groups, so it will be easier for me to explain them to you."

Andy was a decent tour guide as they made their way through the many levels of the tree trunk. "Munching to your right are the ladybugs. Crunching on your left are the grasshoppers, buzzing overhead are the bees, and fluttering all around us are the butterflies."

Andy stopped to indicate that the tour was over, but Bella interjected. "Where are the rest of the caterpillars?" she asked.

Andy took a bow. "You are looking at the one and only," he said with a smile, "But do you see those butterflies fluttering about?" Bella glanced at the butterflies floating around them and nodded. "Well, rumor has it they were caterpillars yesterday," Andy said.

Bella looked upon Andy in confusion, but he suddenly changed the topic. "Hey, do you have any plans for the rest of today?" he asked.

"I'm not sure," replied Bella. "My friends are waiting for me outside. We are on a spiritual journey."

"It sounds like you and I have a lot in common," said Andy. "I am on a journey as well."

Andy paused for a moment to focus. "Oh, you are Mira's little one," he said, his face lighting up in realization. "I've been expecting you."

"What do you mean?" Bella asked.

"I am here with my guide Lina, and she walks with me on my journey," responded Andy. "This morning, after prayer, Lina told me all about you and asked me to show you around. I got so involved in filling my tummy that the time slipped away from me. Otherwise, I would have met you when you first arrived."

"I wonder why Mira and Gracie did not tell me to look for you," said Bella.

"Our guides prefer that we do some of our path walking on our own, without explanation or suggestion on their part," said Andy. "I'm sure they wanted you to enter this beautiful flowering tree with no expectations."

"Ah, yes, that sounds like Mira," Bella said. "She likes me to have an open mind so that God can come into my heart. What other secrets do you know about our friends?"

Andy laughed, disclosing that all he knew was that they spent a lot of time in that part of the forest.

"I can see why. This is a beautiful place," said Bella.

"Let's get a snack and find a place to rest, and I'll fill you in on what comes next," said Andy.

"I'm up for it," said Bella. "First, let's go back to the butterflies. What did you say about them being caterpillars yesterday?"

Andy stepped closer. "I have no clue," he replied in a whisper. "Like I said, as far as I know, it's just a rumor. A bunch of silliness if you ask me! Now, let's see about that snack."

"Didn't you just eat?" asked Bella.

"Feeding on this plant is different," Andy replied. "I am hungry for Jesus, and God feeds a hungry heart." Bella listened as Andy continued instructing. "But be careful not to eat from a flower or leaf that is not yet ready."

"How do I know which ones are ready?" Bella quickly interrupted.

"Listen to the small voice in your heart, and as you approach, God will guide you," said Andy.

"I'm still learning to listen to that voice," Bella replied.

"All in good time," said Andy. "God has a path for you to follow, and as long as you continue to trust in that voice, He will lead you to new and exciting adventures."

Andy and Bella spent much of the day exploring all of the blessings the tree contained. Eventually, they snuggled in a quiet place where Andy explained how he came to find God in his heart. "Once I learned to give my cares and worries to God," he said, "so many things in my life came together."

"Like what?" Bella asked.

"I learned that my attitude about life was making me unhappy, not my circumstances," Andy explained. "Lina says that as my faith grows, my knowledge will increase. I guess that is what makes this a journey. We learn as we go."

"You have a very positive outlook about it all," said Bella. "I need to work on that."

"I have learned that to stay encouraged, you have to be patient and believe," Andy continued. "God will shine His light on you when you least expect it."

"God's light has been good for me," Bella responded. "He has shown me so many beautiful things through it."

"I have walked a similar path to yours. From what I can see in the short time I've spent with you, my lovely friend, the Lord is turning you into a masterpiece," said Andy.

"How can you be so sure?" Bella asked.

"I see it in your sparkle," Andy pressed on. "When you talk about how God makes you feel, you glow. I recognize that as God within you."

"I have noticed that your glow is always turned on," said Bella.

"It took a lot of time and hard work for my glow to become a part of who I am," replied Andy, "but boy, it was worth it!"

"I would love to hear your story," said Bella, "if you don't mind sharing."

"I think we have some time," Andy replied. "Scoot a little closer, and I'll tell you how God has changed me."

Bella and Andy rested on a fallen leaf while he shared the details about how God had united him with Lina. Bella listened closely and often felt herself hurting for the pain he endured, as it seemed so similar to hers. Andy became emotional several times, but there was a moment when the expression on his face changed from pain to joy.

At that point, Andy became quiet. Bella gave him a couple of minutes and then got up the nerve to keep the conversation going. "Andy, what are you thinking about right now?" she asked.

Andy looked at Bella with a smile. "It feels good to tell someone my story," he admitted. "I have had God and Lina at my side during this journey. Now having met you, everything feels that much better."

"How so?" Bella asked.

"Talking to you is different in that you and I are alike," said Andy. "We understand each other."

"It does feel nice to walk with someone else who has felt what I have felt," said Bella. Suddenly, Bella's mind flooded with questions, as it had a habit of doing. "Hey, how long have you been in the meadow? Do you always feed on this tree? Do you know why God has brought you here?"

"Slow down, little one," replied Andy. "For someone traveling with a snail, you sure do rattle off the questions in a hurry."

Bella figured that Mira must have told Andy to call her little one and did not press Andy for an explanation. "Mira says I'm always eager to get to the bottom of things. It's just how my brain works," she said.

"No worries," replied Andy. "Let's do some walking, and I'll talk if you promise only to listen, no inquiry." Bella nodded and spoke no more while Andy revealed what was in his heart.

Knowing his purpose was to help ignite the fire within Bella's heart, Andy spoke genuinely and with care. "I am here because this is where God led me to be," he said. "Every step and breath allows me to be right where God has planned. God continues to whisper gently in my heart and deep within my soul. His voice reassures me there is no spot where He is not. Best of all," continued Andy, "this lifelong journey is not traveled alone. I trust in God's voice and His never-failing love."

As Andy finished speaking, Bella leaned in for a great big hug. She could not stop the tears from leaving her eyes. Watching her tears fall, Andy asked, "Are you alright?"

"I will be," replied Bella. "Your words were beautiful, and I consider you a blessing. It was brave of you to share with me."

"Not hard to do when you have Jesus as a companion on this road," replied Andy.

This remark confused Bella. "I have not seen a road yet," she said. "I have walked in the dirt, slept in a rock, danced in the mud, and ended up in a tree. Is there an actual road?"

"You'll see soon," replied Andy. "It's the road to our new beginning."

CHAPTER TWELVE
Hide and Seek

"How will we find this road? Can you lead me to it?" Bella asked, eager for the next step in her journey with God.

"I have an idea of where we could start," replied Andy with a smile. "Let's play a game of hide and seek."

"That sounds like fun, but you have been in this tree much longer than I have," said Bella. "I don't think I'll know where to hide or where to find you."

"Silly girl, we are not doing the hiding. God is," said Andy.

"I'm afraid I don't understand," said Bella.

"We need to walk deeper into the tree, and I'll explain it as we go," said Andy.

Andy led Bella through the tree and showed her more fruitful vines and the forest friends feeding on them. Bella appreciated the sights of the blooming flowers and the excitement of all the creatures. Bella was quick to fire off questions to Andy, and he tolerated it well. Andy's responses were clear to Bella, and she considered him an excellent teacher and a great listener.

Suddenly, a team of butterflies interrupted their conversation and began to flutter overhead, startling Bella. "Oh, my, why are those butterflies chasing us?" Bella asked.

"They are not after us. They want us to follow them," responded Andy.

"How can you be so sure? Maybe it's a trap!" exclaimed Bella.

"Did you forget where we are?" Andy asked. "Tap into your courage and trust that God is not leading us into anything we cannot handle." Just then, the butterflies flew past them, and Andy picked up his pace. "Come on, Bella, run with me!" he shouted.

Bella took a deep breath, and in a loud voice, she proclaimed, "I trust the process; I have courage. With God, all things are possible!" Then, before she knew it, all sixteen of Bella's legs were moving as fast as they could. Bella and Andy followed the butterflies for what seemed like hours until suddenly, the butterflies were no longer in sight.

Andy kept running as if he knew where they had gone. "Andy, wait!" Bella shouted. "It's getting hard to keep up with you." In a flash, Andy was out of sight, and Bella looked upon a bright light, different from the light that filled the tree. The glow shone with all sorts of colors. At first, Bella thought the colors were similar to that of a rainbow, but then she realized they looked like the colors on Mira's shell. "Mira, are you in the light?" Bella called out.

Instantly, Bella considered how far they had run and figured that Mira could not have caught up to them, especially at the pace she moved. Wanting another look, she closed her eyes tightly and then opened them again, but nothing had changed. "Andy, are you still here?" she asked. "I can't see anything except that light."

"I'm right here next to you," Andy replied, slowly pushing against her so she could feel his presence.

"Where have the butterflies gone, and what is with that light?" Bella asked.

"The butterflies are part of the hide and seek," said Andy. "God used them to bring us to where He wants us to be. Now it is up to us to do the work and find Him."

"God is very clever in the way He grabs our attention," said Bella.

"You wait, little one, this is only the beginning. Are you ready for the next step?" Andy asked.

"It depends. Do we have to run again?" asked Bella. "All that running has wiped me out."

"It sounds to me like it's time for some living water," Andy said. "Follow me!"

Andy led Bella up and around a hill until they came to a plant with flowers that resembled little saucers. Each flower held shimmering water, just enough for one drink.

"I have never seen flowers in this shape," Bella remarked. "They must be pretty special."

"Watch this," said Andy, and he crawled up into one of the petals and dipped his face in, drinking up all the water. As he lifted his face from the flower, droplets of moisture surrounded his happy expression. "Do I look refreshed?" he asked.

"You look wet!" Bella exclaimed.

"I guess you can't really see the refreshment in my body," said Andy. "I guarantee you, though, God has blessed this water. All who drink from it never thirst."

"How can you be so sure?" questioned Bella.

"Has Mira mentioned God's book to you?" asked Andy.

"Yes, but only briefly. She said I would learn more about that later," replied Bella.

"Lina said the same to me," agreed Andy. "However, from what I understand, it has to do with being spiritually fed. When we drink up all God has to offer us, we will never want for anything else. God's blessings are enough to satisfy us."

"Anything that can satisfy you," chuckled Bella, "must be a blessing!"

"Well, what are you waiting for?" Andy asked. "Jump on in; the water is perfect!" Andy guided Bella from one flower to the next until they were both refreshed and ready to move forward.

As they headed out of the flowers, Bella grew concerned about why God would hide from them in the first place. "Andy, why is God hiding from us?" she asked.

"God isn't hiding," said Andy. "Hide and seek is an exercise to learn how to feel His presence."

"Is this one of the ways Lina has helped you to grow on your journey?" Bella asked.

"Yes," replied Andy. "According to our spiritual guides, this is where we begin our journey to find God in all things. Before we start, let's pray."

"That's the best idea you have had all day," Bella replied.

"Would you like to start us off?" Andy asked.

"No, you go ahead," replied Bella. "I will close my eyes and focus on your words."

With that, Andy began his prayer. "Loving God, we ask that You guide us as we enter onto this new path. Please give us the eyes to see You, ears to hear You, and the wisdom to trust in Your guidance. If things get challenging or unsettling, we ask for courage and strength. Help us to remember You love us and will never leave us. Amen."

Andy was silent for a moment before instructing Bella to open her eyes. Bella's gaze, still lowered, fell onto her feet on the path. "He did it again!" she exclaimed. "I've stepped on a message in the dirt! God has given us a blessing." Careful with her steps, Bella moved to get a closer look.

"What does it say?" Andy asked.

Bella scooted as close as she could without disturbing the dirt underfoot. "Okay, I think I can read it," she said. "It says, 'We walk by faith, not by sight.'[8] It must be a clue for our hide and seek game!"

"Yep," said Andy. "The next step for us today is a faith walk."

"What is a faith walk?" Bella asked.

"We participate by using all of those gifts we asked God for in our prayer," replied Andy.

"Can you explain how that works?" asked Bella, still a little confused.

"Gladly," said Andy. "To find God in all things, we need to learn how to trust that He is always there, even when we can't physically see Him. We will do this by using our faith, and not our eyes, to navigate the path."

"It all sounds impossible to do with our eyes closed," said Bella.

"Nothing is impossible with God,"[9] said Andy. "Let's not forget where our blessings come from. Anything we do, we do in harmony with God, even with our eyes closed."

"I wish I had your confidence," said Bella.

"I know you have courage inside you, Bella," said Andy. "It's a matter of letting God in to guide you. Close your eyes now, and rely on God."

"Rely on God," Bella echoed. "Amazing things happen through God when I close my eyes."

Andy waited until Bella felt comfortable, and then they began to move forward; Bella kept her eyes closed. Shortly after the first couple of steps, Andy instructed Bella to listen for God's whispers and reminded her of the words in the dirt.

Bella began to move and quietly recited, "We walk by faith, not by sight.[10] Trust the process. I can do all things through Christ."[11]

"Magnificent, Bella," said Andy. "Keep going and whisper to God, 'Enlighten the eyes of my heart, Lord.'"[12] Bella's heart quickened, and she became more confident in her steps.

"I'm doing it, Andy! I am doing it," she cried out. "I'm walking blind. My heart is filling up with faith and trust in God."

"Tell me what it feels like," replied Andy.

"I feel warm, and my body is alive! It's funny; I don't feel afraid anymore," she exclaimed.

"Stay in the course, Bella," Andy instructed. "Don't stop until you sense that Jesus has come completely into your heart."

"How will I know? How will He get there? What does it feel like to have Jesus in your heart?" Bella asked.

"There you go with the rapid-fire questions again," Andy replied. "Trust in God, and when it happens, you will know."

Andy stayed close as Bella continued on her walk of faith. He kissed prayers up for each step she took, asking God to open her heart. Andy had already taken his walk of faith and knew what to watch for in Bella. After a while,

Bella's pace slowed, and her body glowed brighter than ever before.

As this happened, Andy knew her walk was nearly complete. "Bella, do you remember the prayer we said earlier?" he asked.

"Yes," Bella softly responded.

"Kiss it up to God now, from your heart," Andy instructed, "and when you feel Jesus grab hold of it, you can open your eyes."

Bella was confident, but she needed more instruction. "Do I keep walking while I pray, or do I need to stop?" she asked.

"Keep moving. We are nearly there," Andy replied.

"Okay, here it goes!" Bella said gleefully. "God, please guide me as I begin on a new path. Open my eyes, ears, and heart so that I learn to trust You. I know I will need Your courage and strength, so I thank You in advance for those gifts. I know You will always be there, and I am never alone. Amen."

As Bella concluded her prayer, she forgot what Andy wanted her to do next. So, she relaxed her mind and let it wander as she continued the mindful walk. As she did, God provided her with beautiful images of the emotions in her heart. She saw Jesus smiling at her, often surrounded by glistening streams. His smile was unlike anything she had seen before.

Before long, Bella could hear the sounds of water and feel the warmth of a meadow breeze. She continued to walk at a steady pace, and the warm wind on the water helped guide her. In one unshaken breath, glittering tears fell from her eyes, and she could hear a voice whisper, "Follow Me." As she let the breath back out, she felt herself come to a stop.

"Andy," Bella called out. "I saw the face of God, and I heard His voice. I felt His breath in the wind."

"I know. I can see it all over you. Open your eyes and take a look," Andy replied. Bella dried her eyes, and as they opened, she found herself standing at the edge of a waterfall flowing into a beautiful pond. Bella fixed her gaze on her reflection in the water, noticing her appearance had changed. She was speechless at the sight of herself.

It had been so long since her colors had faded, and now they shined brighter than ever before. Andy saw her gaze and spoke up. "It looks to me like you are filled with hope," he said.

"I like the way hope looks on me," replied Bella.

"Come close, let's pray," said Andy. Andy held Bella close, and they quietly offered a prayer of gratitude to God.

Andy and Bella were grateful to God for the events of their day, and they made that known in the way they prayed. Following this, Andy recommended that they enjoy the landscape of the pond surrounding them. He was hoping to get Bella to open up about how she was feeling. "How are you, Bella?" he asked.

"Well," she responded, "I thought for sure I would be exhausted after all the walking and running we did. Surprisingly though, I am not tired at all. I feel energized and restored, almost like I have been made new."

"New is nice, and it's just the beginning," said Andy.

Bella was very pleased with all that happened and looked forward to what Andy implied. There was something still puzzling her, though. *Where did the butterflies go?* she pondered.

CHAPTER THIRTEEN
Friendly Yellow

"Come on, Bella, it's time to show off those colors!" said Andy. He insisted on celebrating the completion of Bella's faith walk, so, eager to please him, she let her thoughts about the butterflies go for the time being.

"How do you propose we do that?" Bella asked.

"I'll announce you to the meadow while you parade yourself around the pond," Andy replied. "Hello! All in the meadow! Come and see!"[13] As the other creatures inside the tree gathered in response, Bella beamed with excitement and sauntered around the pond.

"Look at me!" Bella exclaimed. "I gave God my heart, and it shows! I want the birds and all the forest friends to hear me. Oh, butterflies, where have you gone? Look at me now!"

Bella continued to run circles around the pond, praising God and loving her moment while Andy took pleasure in her joy. All the others feeding in nearby bushes came to the water's edge to take part in the celebration.

"Come forward, everyone," said Andy. "Let us welcome Bella into God's light as a newly blessed member of the Royal Forest." Bella, surprised by how formally Andy was treating the situation, wished Mira was there to see it all happening. Andy looked like he was enjoying the attention, so Bella allowed him to continue.

"My friends of the forest," announced Andy, "I have seen this little one allow God into her heart. Before my very eyes, she held onto her hope and allowed the light of the

Spirit to shine. Bella, we are grateful to you for sharing your celebration with us today. In participation with you," Andy continued, "I have been strengthened and encouraged. Accompanying you toward a new path has given me much joy."

Suddenly, Andy lost his words, and Bella noticed something extraordinary occurring. "Andy," she called out. "You might want to take a look at your reflection." At Bella's insistence, Andy went to the water and carefully leaned forward to look at himself.

"Bella, can you please join me at the water's edge?" Andy asked.

Bella looked out to those still assembled in the crowd. "Sit tight," she told them. "We will be right back."

"Andy, is everything okay?" Bella whispered when she reached him. Andy had an embarrassed look about him.

"I appear to have changed slightly, and I don't want the group to see me this way," Andy admitted. Bella thought Andy was beautiful and wondered if this had ever happened to him before.

"Andy, you are stunning! You should be proud of your appearance," Bella reassured him. "God has decorated you in royal blue with golden pearls. Why would you want to hide this?"

"Oh, Bella, these pearls make me look funny," replied Andy.

"They do not," said Bella. "You are silly. I watched those pearls appear on you while you were sharing how our experience made you feel. It seems to me that this is God's way of allowing you to show everyone that you carry Him in your heart. You did not have any issues announcing my outward changes. I think you ought to be just as proud of yours."

"Lina said this would happen one day, and I should embrace it. But, Bella, I don't look much like a caterpillar anymore," replied Andy.

"You look just as God has intended," said Bella. "You are beautiful in His sight! If you ask me, I think you look very smart!" she exclaimed.

"Are you implying that I now have pearls of wisdom?" asked Andy.

"Yes," she replied. "You have helped to renew me by leading me closer to God. He has rewarded you with golden pearls! Now, how about we get back to the group?" Bella said.

As they approached the spot where they'd left the group, Bella was the first to notice something very odd. "Um, Andy, how long do you think we were away?"

"Long enough for the crowd to disappear, apparently," chuckled Andy.

"I think it's more than that. God changed the trees while we were gone!" Bella exclaimed.

"Huh?" questioned Andy.

"Stop walking and look up," Bella whispered. "I think this is the handiwork of our God Squad." Swiftly, Bella pushed Andy behind a large mushroom, where they could peek at what was happening near the rocks.

"Hey!" said Andy. "Be careful not to break off any of my pearls."

"Shush, they will hear you," said Bella.

"I don't see anyone there," said Andy. "I think you have left your mind near the water." Bella gave Andy a stern glance, forcing him to quiet down. In doing so, he noticed a lot of activity going on under the trees and in the rocks.

"Look at all that is happening," whispered Bella. They watched the creatures of the forest work in teams; the birds added silken ribbons to the trees while those on the ground prepared large baskets of food. Many gathered flowers of all colors and spread the petals to outline a path. "This was already a beautiful place, but now it's truly God-kissed."

Andy tried his best to keep his tummy quiet during this time, but watching the food preparation was not helping. "Can we eat now?" he asked.

"Not yet," replied Bella. "I think I see Mira and Gracie. Bella stuck her head out a little further from the mushroom to get a better look. "It's my girls! They have come to find me!"

Bella wanted to run up to them, but Andy held her back. "Wait, Bella. You'll ruin the surprise."

Bella whipped her head around, staring Andy in the eyes. "A surprise? What surprise? Andy, what is going on? What are you not telling me?"

"Slow down, tiger, let's hang out from a distance a bit longer," he replied. Bella did not appreciate him beating around the bush and let him know by quickly tapping all sixteen of her feet in an upset manner.

Andy knew that Bella was serious and gave up on holding back the truth any longer. "Okay, okay, still your feet, little one, and I'll confess," he said.

"Out with it!" shouted Bella.

"Well, I was supposed to distract you, and when God gave me the pearls, it actually became the perfect opportunity," said Andy.

"Distract me? Why?" asked Bella.

"Our guides have something special for you," replied Andy. "If we go back too soon, they will not be ready."

"Well then, what are we supposed to do?" asked Bella.

"We wait for the signal," replied Andy.

In the meantime, Andy allowed Bella to peer out and watch the formation unfolding before them. Mira was leading everyone in an orchestrated way so that every detail was perfect. Bella watched as the grasshoppers worked together with the ladybugs to gather rocks. They carried a pile over to the bees, who then directed where to place each one. Andy quickly remembered what was coming next, and, not wanting to ruin it for Bella, he thought it best to divert her attention.

"Hey, Bella," he said. "I don't think I can control my hunger noises anymore. If we don't do something about it quickly, they will find us sneaking a peek."

"I don't want to miss any of this," Bella replied. "Grab a hunk of grass; that should hold you over."

This is not working, Andy thought, and he decided to take matters into his own hands. In one big burst, Andy gave Bella a friendly shove. Bella flew off her feet and into a patch of bright yellow dandelions. She took a moment to compose herself, then escaped the yellow mess calm, cool, and collected. Even so, Andy could tell she was not a happy camper.

"Ha-ha! Look at you! You are all yellow!" he yelled with uncontrollable laughter.

Bella wanted to respond in anger, but her mood quickly shifted when a breeze blew in, triggering the yellow particles to blow directly at Andy. "Who's laughing now?" Bella chuckled.

Oh, it worked! thought Andy. Happy that he had been able to distract Bella, the two of them rolled around in the grass, leaving a trail of yellow dust everywhere.

While rolling around the meadow, Bella had nearly forgotten about the surprise awaiting her until a musical note from within the trees startled her. "Andy," she said, "is that the signal?"

"Um, maybe," replied Andy. "I suggest we wait and listen. I promise we will know when it's time." Bella did not know what to do. The first thing that came to her mind was to pray. She wandered just a little further from the dandelions and quieted herself.

"God," she said, "only You know what is coming next, and I promise to trust in You. I am grateful to You for Andy and all my new friends. Please, God, calm the restlessness and allow me to be brave in facing the unknown. Amen."

Andy had been watching Bella, and when he saw that her eyes were open, he let out a forced sneeze. Quickly, he placed a hand over his mouth, alerting Bella of his concern that he gave away their location. Just then, musical notes began whistling through the trees. Bella recognized the sound and spoke up.

"Gracie!" she exclaimed, glancing at Andy for confirmation. "Gracie is the signal; I know it! Let's go!" Bella wanted to run through the trees as quickly as possible, but Andy held her back.

"Remember," he said, "they don't know that you know!"

"I promise not to give it away," Bella said. Together, they rolled down the hill, through the trees, and landed right on Mira's back. In a quick burst, Bella and Andy slid off Mira and tried to compose themselves.

"I see God is tossing blessings from the sky again," Mira said happily.

"Sorry about that," said Andy. "Momentum got the best of us."

"No worries," replied Mira. "Andy, if you would take your place, I'd like to have a moment with Bella."

Bella gave Andy a wink, letting him know that she would not tell Mira anything about ruining the surprise. Andy was still joyful, knowing that he had not shared every detail of it with Bella. Andy joined Gracie and Lina while Mira stepped back to take in Bella's beauty.

"I knew it was possible, but I had to see it for myself," Mira said. "You are quite the sight! Yellow looks good on you."

"It's friendly yellow," Bella replied with a laugh. "I had a moment with a dandelion."

"I'm looking beyond that, my dear," said Mira. "I see God's restoring grace." Bella rushed to Mira's side, and together they shared happy and blessed tears. Bella's heart was bursting to tell Mira about everything that happened to her, but all she could get out were tears of joy. "Come now, little one," said Mira. "Your time is now."

CHAPTER FOURTEEN
Made to Glow

If ever there was a time when Bella wanted to move at a snail's pace, this was it. Bella allowed the music to guide her through the trees while Mira followed close behind. Everything Bella had seen from a distance had changed. The ribbons strung throughout the trees illuminated the sky, and the rocks that those watching were sitting upon glowed. "Go slowly and take it all in," whispered Mira.

Bella felt her breath quicken in the excitement of the moment but forced herself to pause and view her surroundings. She closed her eyes and took in a deep breath, intending to focus on the moment when her gaze returned. However, God had other plans.

Gently and with purpose, Bella allowed her eyes to open and found herself surrounded by a cloud of glittering butterflies. She could not focus on just one; there were so many, and they were blocking her view of everything else ahead of her. The beauty that the butterflies created around Bella was stunning, and nothing else mattered to her.

"I wondered where you all had gone," said Bella. "I suppose you are part of God's plan for whatever I am walking into?" At the sound of Bella's voice, the butterflies changed how they were flying, organizing themselves in such a way that one stood out from the rest. This butterfly was the most spectacular butterfly Bella had ever seen. The butterfly flew in a divinely graceful manner, different from the others. The presence of such a butterfly had dazzling effects, leaving Bella speechless.

Soon, the air filled with an angelic voice as the butterfly began to speak. "You have been through many trials, my precious child, but your persistence and faith kept you going. Your dedication to prayer has allowed you to quiet your mind and hear the voice of God." The butterfly paused for a moment and motioned for Mira to stand alongside Bella.

"My dear little one," said Mira, "you have traveled a long journey and given your heart to God. His light now shines on you for the world to see." Then, the butterfly perched herself upon Mira's back, the exact spot where Bella had landed during her storm. In doing so, the butterfly was eye to eye with Bella, and this brought Bella out of her trance.

"Allow me to introduce myself," the butterfly said. "I am Lina, and I am fortunate to meet you." Bella stared into Lina's eyes before stepping back slightly and saw a striking resemblance to Andy.

Finally, Bella was able to speak. "You are Andy's Lina," she said. "I can see it. The golden pearls on your wings are the same ones Andy received as a gift."

"You are very observant, little one," replied Lina.

"Are you the leader of the butterflies?" Bella asked.

"No, my child, God leads," Lina said. "My job is to be a companion and make sure everyone stays on task."

"Speaking of staying on task," Mira chimed in, "we should probably get moving."

"Oh!" Bella shouted, "Finally, a snail in a hurry!"

"Don't get too used to it," Mira responded as they all shared a heartfelt laugh. However, their amusement came to a stop when the distant music grew louder and the light around them brightened. Though absent from her sight, Bella could hear someone singing. Not wanting to miss a beat, Bella promptly looked to Lina and Mira for direction.

"Walk in God's light," directed Lina.

"Let go and let God in, little one," Mira instructed.

Mira and Lina moved ahead of Bella, guiding her to the gathering spot. Bella allowed herself to move slowly and take in everything around her. She could see Andy in the distance with a fat smile and grass dangling from his chin. At first, Bella could not make out where the singing was coming from, but as she got closer, what she saw brought joyful tears to her eyes.

Dottie and her family sat upon the glowing rocks singing their little hearts out. Gracie and many other grasshoppers provided music like a magnificent orchestra. *The only ones missing*, thought Bella, *are the fireflies.*

In one sudden swoop, the fireflies appeared and began to dance around the rocks. "God is listening to my thoughts again," Bella murmured under her breath. Bella's happiness showed in her smile, and this was pleasing to Mira, Lina, and Andy, who continued to gaze upon her.

As the radiant music faded out, the fireflies guided Bella to a heart-shaped rock painted in the colors of the rainbow. Bella was eager to have a seat, but before she could, the fireflies hovered over her rock. After a moment, they separated, allowing Bella a glance. Written on her rock in glitter was the word "Hope." Bella was grateful to the fireflies for the heartfelt expression and nodded to God in acknowledgment.

Seated alongside Bella was Andy; his rock was a lovely shade of blue adorned with golden pearls, and on it was the word "Faith." Mira's rock stood tall and shimmered just like her shell. Lina hovered over her rock, which she only needed for resting her wings, and Gracie's rock was nestled in a thick patch of grass.

I wonder, thought Bella. *Andy has become like Lina, and the other grasshoppers resemble Gracie. Could it be that one day I will become like Mira?* Other thoughts also popped into Bella's head. It took all her strength to contain her questions until an appropriate time.

Instead, Bella sent her thoughts back into the present moment. She admired all that was around her. It was so lovely to see Dottie and her family sitting amongst them, and Gracie sure did know how to lead a very talented musical group. Bella allowed just one thought to pop out of her mouth. Trying her best not to slip from her rock, she leaned into Andy and whispered, "What's next?"

"I don't know. This part is a first for me," Andy replied.

"You mean you have never seen anything like this happen before?" Bella asked.

"Nope, and Lina did not tell me what to expect either," he said.

Before Bella could ask any more questions, Mira stood upon her rock and rang a bell. The sound of the chime was gentle yet provided direction for all to settle in silence. Standing as tall as possible on her rock, Mira instructed all those gathered to allow God to enter their hearts. Once they were quiet, she led them in a prayer to the Holy Spirit.

"Let us remind ourselves that we are in the presence of God," she began. "Come Holy Spirit, take away our jitters, and help us to relax. Replace our troubles with heavenly peace. Substitute gentle courage for the anxiety within us. Remove our fear through our strong faith."

Mira paused briefly before asking everyone to stand and position themselves in the direction of Bella and Andy. Bella was not too sure what to think of that, but she allowed herself to embrace the moment. She peeked over at Andy, who had his head bowed, and did the same. They listened carefully to the prayer's conclusion. "Let us take in all that You are and be healed according to Your Word. Amen."

What happened next was a shock at first to Bella and Andy, as well as a blessed moment neither would soon forget. Mira motioned for Lina, Gracie, and Dottie to join her while Lina fluttered her wings to address the crowd.

"In your journeys, you have witnessed the power of God in all things," Lina said. "We have asked you here today to join us in celebrating the renewed faith of Andy and Bella."

Lina then flew aside, and Dottie came forward to say a few words. It seemed it was a bit of a struggle for her to see everyone, so Mira slid over, allowing Dottie to climb atop her shell. Seeing all the eyes peering back at her, Dottie grew nervous. Gracie sensed Dottie's fear and softly played a calming hymn.

The music eased Dottie enough to share all she knew about Bella and the lovely things she had learned about Andy. Dottie was grateful to the God Squad for welcoming her among them and gave praise to God for allowing her to walk in His light. Concluding her reflection, she slid down from Mira, who was ready to offer her testimony.

"Accompanying Bella on her path of renewed faith and preparing for her transformation was a gift," Mira said. "Similarly, Lina has experienced the wonders of Andy's renewing travels. Today we gather to share in the celebration with them. In a moment, we will ask Andy and Bella to step forward and share the fruits of their journeys with you."

Instantly overcome by fear, Bella's ears fell deaf to Mira's voice. Needing an explanation, and fast, she turned to Andy. "Mira has most certainly flipped her shell," Bella grumbled while nudging into Andy's side. "I cannot go up there and share my story. On top of that, I don't understand all this talk about transformation."

Andy, in a comforting way, tried to ease Bella's anxious heart, "Focus on what we have learned on our travels. Allow God's Word to carry you, for you can do all things through Him. I witnessed your courage and persistence as you blindly trusted in God. Tap into that power now and show them your courage, little one."

Following Andy's pep talk, Bella's face still showed unease. Andy knew that it was up to him to step in and lead by example. "I'll go first, and you follow my lead," he said. Then, putting on a brave face, Andy abruptly got up, interrupted Mira's speech, and moved to the group's center. Lina fluttered overhead, gazing down upon him as he began to speak.

"Hello! Many have said that I look like I have been well-fed in the forest. I guess it's my plump figure that gives me away." Andy's humor prompted an immediate response of laughter, and given the smile Bella was wearing, he knew a chuckle was what she needed to relax.

"In all honesty," he went on, "the nourishment that matters most to me is that which I have received from God.

I began on my path broken and brittle, until I bumped into Lina. Not many have walked directly into a flying insect, but I managed to do it. That miraculous day, the day that I closed my eyes in my despair, Lina swooped in and caught me. It wasn't until later that I learned God arranged for her to find me."

Lina, still fluttering overhead, listened proudly as her companion shared his heart. "God sent Lina," he continued, "to protect, guide, and lead me into a better relationship with Him. I am happy to report that God and I are very close now, and I cannot get enough of His spiritual food. You are looking at one caterpillar who is hungry for Jesus!"

Immediately, those gathered sprang from their seats in applause. Andy drew in his belly before leaning forward to take a big bow. As he did, the weight of his body forced him into a ball. All curled up, Andy rolled down the aisle before stopping at Bella's feet.

While slowly unraveling himself, Andy's eyes met Bella's, and he gave her a friendly wink. Reciprocating with a thankful grin, Bella reached down to help him up. "That was quite the show!" she exclaimed. "You may want to add public speaking to your list of spiritual gifts!"

"Oh, it was nothing," replied Andy. "I was quite nervous at first, and that's when my humor took over. I often use silliness to overcome my fears."

"I'd say it worked wonders," said Bella. "You did not appear nervous at all and spoke with ease. God's light looks great on you! In fact, my friend, you were made to glow!"

CHAPTER FIFTEEN
God's Word

Applause echoed through the forest as Andy returned to his rock. Bella welcomed him next to her and leaned her head gently against his.

"I know you are frightened, little one," he said in a soft voice, "but it's not as bad as it seems. Trust me, and trust that God will be right there with you." Bella's eyes were on the verge of letting tears flood when they met Andy's eyes again.

"Andy," she said, "I need you to pray for me while I'm up there. It's the only way I know I can do this."

"I'd be happy to," replied Andy.

"You looked so calm up there," said Bella. "I can't make my body stop quivering."

"As you approach the center, I want you to pause and, in that exact moment, ask God to join you," replied Andy. "I will kiss up a prayer at the same time. God will send all the words to your heart and onto your lips."

Still feeling squeamish, Bella focused on Andy's suggestions and arose from her rock. Moving in a snail-like manner, she gravitated toward the center where Mira was waiting.

"You can do this. Walk mindfully and pause in the center," she whispered. Bella's steps were careful; she wanted to be sure to pause when Andy was ready to pray. As Bella fixed her gaze ahead, her eyes met Mira, and they exchanged a hopeful expression.

The look on Mira's face filled Bella with confidence. In one last step forward, Bella stood still and asked God to meet her. There she waited, vulnerable and hopeful that God would hold her and grace her with the courage needed.

Bella realized that she needed to find a way to calm her heart before it beat completely out of her chest. *If I am going to do this, I need a calm spirit*, she thought. *I will ask the group for their help.* As she was gathering the courage to involve those around her, she suddenly heard a crunching noise. Bella's eyes immediately shifted to where the noise was coming from, and there sat Andy with his cheeks stuffed with grass.

Andy's humor provided a sense of calm within Bella, and it gave her a quick moment to gather her thoughts. Just then, Bella had an idea of how to show others how to find God in the silence.

"Before I begin to share my story," she said, "I wonder if we could take a moment to settle ourselves in the presence of God. Our spiritual guides have taught us that God is often in the stillness, in the places where it is so quiet that you can hear a pin drop. That is where my heart finds God. I invited God into my heart by listening only to His voice. At first, I resisted the quiet times with God. Often, in that space, painful memories found me. But now," she admitted, "my heart and mind are open to what God is calling me towards."

Bella was feeling at ease now that love from God's Word had found its place within her. "God's plan for me is still a little fuzzy. However, I have a sense that it has something to do with being calm, peaceful, and still." At this, Mira and Lina exchanged a glance. Andy, seated nearby, caught onto that and wondered what those two were thinking this time. He kept his eyes on Mira and Lina and listened to Bella as she continued giving her witness.

"The joy I have in my heart for God far outweighs the pain of all I have lost. I can't imagine my life having never landed on Mira's back." The joy on Bella's face was evident to all those who looked upon her. "I am blessed to have traveled with Dottie and heard Gracie's beautiful music," she continued with a chuckle, "and encountered a slight fear of being eaten by Andy."

Not only did Bella laugh at that, but everyone else did as well. Once the laughter subsided, Bella continued. "I have lost so much of my past, but I have gained so much in return. Most of all, I have found a new life with God."

Suddenly, the fireflies buzzed their way through the crowd, glittering the air, trees, and everything in their path. Those gathered broke out into cheerful applause.

Bella was feeling loved, and she embraced the moment given to her as she concluded. "Quietly speak to God and ask Him to search your heart and mind. Let go of anything bothering you or holding you back from being with Him. Remain here in God's presence and allow Him to embrace you."

Bella fell silent and entered a quiet space in her heart. At that moment, everything was still; even the birds paused in the comfort of the trees. Just then, Bella's body began to sway from side to side as if she was being rocked like a baby. She looked out at the crowd and beheld one continuous motion of cradle-like rocking. At this, Bella nodded to Gracie, who began to play her song softly.

Mira scooted herself into the center, inviting Dotty to climb upon her. "We give You thanks," Mira sang gleefully. "Oh, Lord, with our whole heart, we sing Your praise." Those gathered continued to sway and sang along.

Gracie continued to play while the others joined Mira and Dottie in the center to praise God together. They were all happily singing the verses when Andy shouted, "Oh, how I love Jesus!" Bella and the spiritual guides quickly turned to share in Andy's glee, dancing circles around one another. Gracie played various melodies, and the celebration continued well into the night. Feeling playful, Andy held tightly to Bella for a big twirl, but Mira scooted her way in and interrupted.

"I think that it is time to finish our preparations for what comes next," she said. Andy and Bella both stared at Mira with confused faces.

Bella spoke up first, needing clarification. "Did you see what Andy and I just did? I can't think of anything else that would be better than that."

"Yeah, we did a lot today," Andy said in agreement. "What we need is for God to replenish us."

Lina joined them in conversation. "There will be plenty of time for that."

"I don't understand," said Bella. "I feel like our journey ends here. After all, we did just testify to God and celebrated His goodness."

Mira snuggled close to Bella. "You and Andy have both come a long way on your journey, but God is not finished with you yet," she replied. "Tonight, I want each of you to choose your favorite place in the meadow."

"What for?" asked Andy.

"That is where you will rest for the night," replied Lina.

"Any place we like?" asked Bella.

Lina replied, "Yes, any place your heart desires."

Bella and Andy needed no time to consider such a place. "I would like to go to the tree of spiritual fruit!" Andy shouted.

Bella turned toward Mira. "Will you take me to the cave of blessings?" she asked.

"You bet I will!" exclaimed Mira. Before heading off, Mira and Lina had a surprise for Bella and Andy and pulled them aside to present it to them. Tucked underneath a low-growing shrub were two wrapped gifts, each tied with a glowing bow and sparkling ribbons. In unison, Mira and Lina offered the packages to their companions.

"Oh, they are so beautiful! What are they?" asked Bella.

"Everything you've ever wondered about God's Word and His messages is contained under the wrapping," said Mira.

"Go ahead, open them," Lina instructed.

Andy was the first to tear through the ribbons and special wrapping. Bella, on the other hand, delicately and with increasing wonder, carefully removed the decorative coverings. Once opened, the pages felt like silk to Bella's touch. "A Bible! Just for me!" she exclaimed. "I've never seen anything like it. This means the world to me!"

"Agreed! I'm pretty sure I won't be eating this," Andy blurted. "It means far too much to me. There are so many gems and blessings written throughout!"

"Consider this a roadmap for life," said Lina. "Look upon it often and soak in its wisdom."

"I'll treasure it forever!" Bella cheered. "Finally, I have God's Word in the palm of my hands!"

Delighting in their new gifts and ready for whatever came next, they all said their goodbyes and wished one another goodnight. Andy and Lina strolled toward his favorite tree while Bella and Mira traveled to the cave of blessings.

It was not long before they reached the mouth of the cave. "I'll be right outside the opening, and I'll be praying for your rest," said Mira. Bella, with God's Word in hand, turned to enter the cave, and a wonderful light comforted her.

It seems like the fireflies anticipated my arrival, thought Bella. Then, she peacefully moved around the cave, focusing on God's words still sparkling around her. Finally, feeling tired, Bella settled in a comfortable spot and gathered her thoughts for bedtime prayer.

It was customary for Bella to close her eyes when she prayed, as it was a way for her to focus on her words. This time, however, Bella could not take her eyes off the spiritual glow surrounding her. In this spectacular light, Bella noticed the outward changes that God had gifted to her. She positioned herself where she could view all of God's words written upon the cave walls and then began to have a conversation with Him.

"Hello, God. Thank You for this precious time in this holy, happy space. Through this experience, You have shown me more than I could ever have imagined. I am grateful for the gift of color and how You have restored me." The light inside the cave brightened as Bella continued to share with God how the changes made her feel.

"When my emotions are pleasant, my stripes are soft, wide, and long. When I am angry or frustrated, my stripes become short and sharp. The colors of happy or pleasant emotions shine bright and warm, whereas sad and fearful emotions appear washed out and ugly."

Focusing on her outward changes made Bella emotional. Only moments ago, God had given Bella the courage to share her heart with all in the forest. Now, she was grateful for this intimate moment with Him. In love and gratitude, she continued.

"When I feel peaceful about something, I know I am where You want me to be. The closer I get to You, the more vibrant my colors become. I cannot thank You enough for everyone and everything You have placed on my path. God, now that You are part of my life, the way I live each day is forever changed."

Bella grew silent, as she could not keep up with her feelings any longer. Emotionally and physically drained, she held tight to God's special book. As she slept in the presence of God, her body shined brighter than ever.

CHAPTER SIXTEEN
Beautifully Broken

As morning arrived, a familiar scent awakened Bella. It smelled as if she had slept in a flower garden. Anxious to determine where it was coming from, Bella sprang to her feet with her eyes wide open. In the center of the cave stood Mira, surrounded by exquisite roses. Bella was intrigued and confused as to how the flowers had arrived. Just then, one of the flowers started moving across the cave floor. "Whoa!" Bella cried out, and she quickly hurried away from the walking rose.

Mira giggled, and as she did, many more of the roses started moving. "What is happening?" Bella asked. Suddenly, the roses began to dance, some of them even flying through the air. It was at that moment that Bella knew the fireflies must be involved. "Good morning, my friends," she said. "Come on out and let me see you."

All at once, the roses filled with light as the fireflies crawled through them. "It looks like you have all had a busy morning," said Bella. "I am impressed at how quiet you all are. I didn't hear a peep!"

"God gifts His helpers with the grace of being light in flight," said Mira.

"I would say so," replied Bella. "Thank you for the flowers. They are both unexpected and beautiful. I don't understand why you placed them here, though."

"I'm glad you asked," replied Mira. "Today will be a day unlike any other. The peaceful slumber you received last night and the nourishment from the roses this morning are to prepare you for a new adventure. Like many other flowers in the forest, these roses are blessed with living water." Bella suddenly recalled what Andy had said about God's replenishing water.

"That's right!" Bella exclaimed. "Andy said when you drink from a flower containing this gift, you will never thirst. Even so, there are so many here! Are Andy and Lina joining us for nourishment?"

"We will meet up with them later this evening, as the day becomes night," Mira replied. "All of the water you see before you, God meant to be for you." Bella looked around and attempted to count the flowers, but there were too many; it also didn't help that the fireflies were still moving them around.

"I don't see how one caterpillar could drink all the water in these roses," Bella said.

"With God, anything is possible,"[14] replied Mira.

"This sounds like a teaching moment," Bella said.

"Yes," said Mira with a smile. "You are beginning to understand my ways."

Together, they sat among the flowers, watching the fireflies dance. Every so often, Bella got up and replenished herself one rose at a time. Mira was gentle and honest in teaching Bella what God had planned next.

"I know how much you enjoy God's light," said Mira. "There is going to come a time when darkness overshadows the light. It is important that you remain focused on God during this time."

"There was darkness in my storm," replied Bella. "However, now I have God in my heart. Will this make it easier to find God in the darkness?"

"Yes," replied Mira. At that, the fireflies began writing something on the cave floor. Bella grew excited at this new blessing and leaned closer to view it.

"Jesus said, 'I have come as light into the world, that whoever believes in me may not remain in darkness,'"[15] read Bella.

"I would say God's timing with that one was spot on!" Mira exclaimed. "When the time comes, little one, focus on how it feels to have God in your heart. Then, eventually, the darkness will subside, and light will return."

"Is there anything else I need to know?" Bella asked.

"As a matter of fact, there is one other very important lesson," Mira explained. "Do not ever forget or give up who you once were. You needed to go through the storm because that is where God chose to meet you. That part of you will offer a lot to your future self."

"You know, I thought I was getting really good at knowing what you were going to say next," said Bella. "However, you are losing me again with all this instruction about new self and old self. What exactly is going to happen?"

Sensing that Bella needed a little reassurance, Mira turned to address the fireflies. "Let's show Bella what we mean by transformation!" she exclaimed. At Mira's command, the fireflies suddenly went dark and entered Mira's shell, making her giggle. Then, in one glorious moment, the light of the fireflies beamed, revealing a surprise on Mira's shell. Bella stood shocked at what her eyes beheld.

Mira stood beautifully broken and illuminated by the light. Her shell, which until now had always seemed so flawless to Bella, was covered in cracks and chips, illuminated by the light from the fireflies. Bella observed the deepest cuts, thinking they were the most painful. Remarkably, though, the way in which the light shone through the deep ones revealed the most beauty.

"Don't be frightened, little one; the chips and cracks you see have been blessed by God."

"Blessed? How can God bless your wounds?" Bella asked.

"When I received the wounds you see," Mira responded, "they were actually blessings in disguise because they brought me closer to God. Look closely, and see that the more shattered you are, the brighter God's light shines through you."

"I don't understand," she said. "I have seen you shine many times. How is it that I have never observed you this way before?" she asked.

"It's all in God's timing," said Mira. "He reveals the hidden beauty within each of us when the time is right."

Bella remained in awe as Mira explained how she once stood where Bella was and had survived storms of her own. "We all have our troubles. Sometimes they leave scars, but that does not mean God will not restore and renew each one of us. Now and then, the pain we go through begins the process of transformation. The brokenness you see represents weaknesses of the past. The fireflies have illuminated the life, which remains, a life walked in faith and held in God's love and light."

Bella's eyes welled up with tears, and she allowed them to fall as she hesitantly moved toward Mira. "Oh, Mira!" she cried out. "You are so beautiful, but my heart aches for the pain that you must have gone through. God has transformed you beautifully!"

Mira snuggled closer to Bella. "God has a plan for you, my little one," she said. "Soon, you will become beautifully broken, transformed by God's love, and fully restored in His light."

"Do you think I will have scars as pretty as yours?" asked Bella.

"We all heal in different ways," replied Mira. "All you need to know for today is that we are all beautiful in God's eyes."

Then, out of nowhere, Mira broke the seriousness with a loud giggle, and the fireflies went dark again. One by one, they flew from her shell and surrounded Bella, ushering her to the cave entrance.

As they reached the opening, Bella turned for one last look. "Do you think I'll ever return here again?" she asked.

"I believe you will," replied Mira. "Don't be surprised, though, if the next time you are in this place, it holds a different meaning for you."

"Is that because of this transformation I am embarking upon?" Bella asked.

"Yes. I also believe that God has gifted you your cave of blessings as an opportunity for continued growth in this space."

Bella took in a deep breath and, upon its release, indicated she was ready to move forward. Mira and the fireflies led Bella a little way down the path until they came to the pond. As they arrived, the sun had just come up over the treetops, and there was a slight mist in the air. They all took a moment to embrace the beauty that God had provided before Bella spoke up.

"I love this place," she remarked. "There is something about the sound of the water that lights me up." In a flash, the fireflies lit up, allowing Bella to see her reflection clearly in the water.

"Take a look at yourself and tell me what you see," Mira instructed.

"I see the light surrounding me, but not within me," she replied. "How can that be? I can feel God's light in my heart. I know it's there."

"You have accepted God into your heart, but the transformation is not yet complete," replied Mira.

"Please tell me what I need to do," said Bella.

"Slow down," replied Mira. "We don't need an anxious caterpillar on our hands today of all days. Let's spend more time admiring the beauty here, and I'll explain."

Bella willingly listened as Mira continued to instruct her. "In order to be reborn, you must lose yourself first," Mira said.

"It sounds like my new journey will be a struggle," said Bella.

"Remember, little one; the struggle is often necessary to become who God meant you to be," Mira replied. "You will draw strength from God when it becomes difficult. However, you will still need to draw power from within to make it happen."

"What's going to happen to me?" asked Bella, still fearful of what was to come.

"Something spectacular!" exclaimed Mira.

Mira and Bella went on, walking and talking nearly the whole day before stopping at a clearing in the forest. Bella thought perhaps it was a secret garden. She admired the lush green grass and the intricately shaped leaves on the trees. Quietly, Bella took in all this new spot had to offer.

It's all so peaceful, she thought. Suddenly, a loud rustling noise broke the silence. A nearby bush was shaking back and forth, and a loud crunching sound came from its roots. "I know that sound," said Bella, and she darted into the bush.

"Hiya, little one!" shouted Andy.

"I knew that noise was you," said Bella. "I can see you didn't starve during the night."

"Nope, I've been well-fed," replied Andy. "Are you hungry?"

"Mira filled me up with water from the roses," replied Bella. "I'm feeling as fat and happy as you look."

As Bella and Andy laughed, Mira and Lina called for them. As Andy and Bella began to make their way out from the inside of the bush, he shared with Bella all he thought she needed to know.

"Okay, now I don't want to cause alarm, but how do you feel about butterflies?" Andy asked.

"You are silly; that does not alarm me. I love butterflies!" cheered Bella.

"Oh, I'm relieved to hear that," said Andy. "We are about to become them!"

CHAPTER SEVENTEEN
Your Wings Are Ready

In that instant, Bella's colors switched from friendly yellow to washed-out green. All sorts of conversations from her journey started to flood Bella's mind, and the word "transformation" shone brightly in each one. Perhaps the most important thing she remembered was the conversation she'd had with Andy when they first met. "They were caterpillars yesterday," she recalled him saying. Worried that Bella was going to be green for a while, Andy attempted to talk her out of her trance.

"How are we doing?" Andy asked. "I expected you to overflow with your rapid-fire questions by now. You know I would never let anyone or anything harm you, right?"

"Uh-huh," Bella responded meekly, still stuck in a green daze.

"And you know that you can trust our spiritual companions and me as well?" Andy asked.

"Uh-huh," Bella murmured.

"Most importantly, Bella, I know you trust God and His will for your life. So that is where I need your mind to go right now," Andy advised.

Andy's last statement brought Bella out of her haze, filling her face with much-needed color. Andy reassured Bella that God had big things in store for them and would protect them along the way. He shared Lina's insights about how glorious it would feel to surrender to God. Bella, in turn, shared Mira's insights about listening for God when the darkness was upon them.

Andy wanted to offer one more suggestion before anything else happened. "Let's dig into God's Word," he said, "and seek His wisdom."

"Do you think it will help?" Bella asked.

"I know it will," Andy said confidently. Bella inhaled a deep breath, taking out her ornate book and allowing it to fall open in her hands. Andy looked over her shoulder and read aloud the message from the page, "'When I am afraid, I put my trust in you.'[16] Wow! Pretty powerful if you ask me."

"It doesn't get much better than that," Bella agreed. "A simple message, yet one that is needed for us to finish what God has asked us to do."

"God knew what we needed, and He gave it to us!" exclaimed Andy. "God is good!"

"Indeed He is!" shouted Bella. Satisfied and convinced that everything they had learned up to this point was supplied and intended by God, Bella and Andy exited the opening of the bush.

Once they were outside, Andy shouted, "I'm ready! Give me wings to fly!"

"In God's time," Lina responded.

"Patience will be essential," Mira chimed in. In her excitement, Bella wanted to speak up, but suddenly she felt very sluggish. Quickly spotting a nearby branch, she laid herself down.

"Is something wrong?" Andy asked as he hurried to her side.

"I'm not sure," replied Bella. "All of a sudden, I can't keep my eyes open." Andy stood still for only a moment when he began to feel the same way.

"You look comfortable," said Andy. "Is there room for two?"

Bella made room beside her, and they rested peacefully while Mira and Lina situated themselves nearby.

"I have never felt like this before," said Bella.

"I'd imagine this is the beginning of our change," said Andy.

Sensing there was not much time before she drifted to sleep, Bella called out to be sure Mira was still there. "Mira, can you hear me?"

"Yes, my child. I hear you, and I will be here throughout this process."

"I'm tired. Do you think I'm ready for this?" asked Bella. She could sense Mira's nod.

"Rest, little one," Mira reassured her. "Very soon, God will draw you toward courage and strength."

Bella's faith and her trust in God allowed her mind to settle. Mira and Lina guarded and prayed for their companions; before long, they saw changes occurring. Andy and Bella had each spun white silk, which they used to attach themselves to their branch.

"Andy," Bella called out, "will we be together when this is over?"

"In my heart, I feel God will keep us together as long as it is necessary," responded Andy.

Just then, they heard soft voices from below. "Be still in your surrender, and breathe in God's Word and light," Mira and Lina whispered.

Mira and Lina's words provided some comfort; however, Bella still felt the need to pray. "Loving God," she began, "I know that I am here now because it is where You have placed me. I am willing to accept Your plan for my life, and I surrender to Your will. Even though I do not know what the future holds, my renewed faith in You enables me to surrender."

Bella hushed her words as a gentle breeze swayed her from side to side. The space which held Bella felt different, and she needed to make adjustments in order to fit within its walls. Having completely surrendered, Bella felt no control over herself. The only thing she knew to do was to let go and allow God to change her.

As she settled herself in the space she'd built, Bella heard the quietest whisper. "When you emerge, My little one, you will have wings to fly." A warmth settled in Bella's heart as she recognized God's whisper.

"It makes so much sense," she said. "I am a child of God! God found His way to me through others. Each time I was called little one, God was calling me."

Beautiful and inspiring thoughts began to bubble up within Bella's heart. Happily, she devoted time in her chrysalis to counting her blessings and recalling moments and places on her journey that had brought her closer to God. As Bella contemplated this place of peace, she gained clarity and understanding of everything she experienced, and she accepted that her storm was actually a very beautiful beginning. Abruptly, a whisper in the dark interrupted her once more. "Dear Bella, now that you have allowed My light into your heart, you are no longer lost. In your surrender, you have found peace. Fly, My little one, and share the good news."

As Bella let those words soak into her mind, her body quickly became accustomed to the gentle movement of her chrysalis.

In the stillness, Bella and Andy rested while their transformation in the chrysalis continued. Mira and Lina remained underneath the branch, where, hour by hour, they prayed, fasted, and dedicated themselves to serving God by protecting His children.

After many days and hours of praying faithfully, Andy's chrysalis started to wiggle, and Lina kissed a prayer up to God.

"Dear God, I ask that You give Andy the strength he needs in this, his most precious struggle. Provide him the gift of perseverance to fight his way through. Amen."

Suddenly, the side of Andy's chrysalis broke open. Slowly, out crawled a beautiful butterfly. It was not long before the butterfly was able to stretch up to the top of where the chrysalis hung. This provided stability and allowed his wings to fall open. At that moment, a glorious light shone upon him.

The light revealed large royal blue and golden beads framing his wings. Shades of green covered the rest of his wings. As it became apparent that Andy's transformation had been successful, Lina lifted up a prayer of gratitude. Mira and Lina delighted in how brightly God had colored Andy, as well as how evident it was that he had taken on many of Lina's attributes. Noticeably, too, God had not changed his appetite. It only took moments for Andy to turn and feed on a nearby flower.

As Andy filled his tummy, Bella remained in her chrysalis, and Mira kept a very close watch. It was not long before Bella's chrysalis began to shake; again, Mira and Lina kissed a prayer up to God. As they prayed, a large crack emerged in the side of Bella's chrysalis. The chrysalis shook forcefully; it was evident that the struggle to break free was very difficult. Concerned for his friend, Andy flew from his perch and settled upon the branch just above the chrysalis. Mira and Lina prayed silently for a safe emergence and watched in awe of what was happening. All in one moment, the sky became a brilliant blue, and nestled in the clouds was a glorious rainbow.

"Oh, my!" shouted Andy. "Look how God has defined the sky!"

"It's like nothing I have ever seen before," said Mira.

"Bella asked for color. It looks to me like God is giving her plenty," said Lina.

Just then, Bella slowly emerged; as she came into view, it was clear she had a small tear on one of her wings. God had transformed her but left a scar. However, the scar was radiant, and the broken wing allowed more of God's light to shine through.

"Is she going to be okay?" asked Andy.

"Yes," replied Mira. "Together with her freshly renewed faith and the strength God has instilled within her, that scar will shine."

They continued to watch as Bella stretched her legs to hang from the branch. As she allowed her wings to fall open, she glistened. Mira, Lina, and Andy stayed close by as Bella worked to regain her strength.

It took some time for both Andy and Bella to become accustomed to their new forms, but when they did, the light surrounding them was as bright as a star. Bella and Andy glowed in the heavenly light, instilling joy in the hearts of their companions.

CHAPTER EIGHTEEN
Let Your Light Shine

A few days after emerging, Mira and Lina prepared to formally present Bella and Andy to those in the meadows of the Royal Forest. Lacking the wings to fly, Mira went a day ahead of the others to make the necessary preparations.

Knowing Bella would be eager to return, Gracie assisted in leading everyone to Bella's favorite pond. The area surrounding the pond bloomed with flowers, and the waterfall brilliantly spilled over, revealing God's beauty. Gracie played her song as Dottie and the others eagerly watched the skies for the butterflies' arrival.

Soon enough, Lina and a cloud of butterflies emerged through the flowers. The butterflies flew together, giving the appearance that they were all connected. All at once, they separated, and Bella and Andy emerged from the center. Everyone watched in awe. Bella sparkled and glowed, just as she had hoped, and Andy was recognizably plump and happy.

Mira instructed all to be silent and welcomed the newly transformed butterflies to her side. "My little ones, what you have received as a gift, you will give as a gift. Go with the Spirit where God places you."

Mira stepped aside to allow Lina to speak. "Dear friends," she said, "God always knew what you would become. Have confidence in your gifts, and remember that Jesus is your compass." Lina moved away from the path, leaving Bella and Andy in the spotlight.

"This is it," said Andy. "Your time to shine."

"No!" said Bella, still hesitant about speeches. "You go first."

"Not a chance," he replied. "This moment is all yours!"

"But what if I make a mistake?" Bella asked.

"You are doing God's work," said Andy. "There are no mistakes, only hiccups." Andy knew that he was also doing God's work in allowing Bella's confidence to grow, and there was no time like the present.

Bella hovered over the path. It was illuminated in light: God's light, shaped like a cross, just as she'd seen on her journey with Mira. Closing her eyes to remember what it felt like in the stillness, Bella began a prayer for all to hear.

"Lord, I ask that You breathe into me Your Spirit for ministering to others. Grace me with all I need to use my spiritual gifts for Your greater good and as spiritual food for those I meet. May my thoughts and phrases be transformed into spiritual wonders. Help me know the pure joy that only comes from Your love. Amen."

Bella opened her eyes and allowed tears of blessings to fall across her cheeks. Stunned by the outpouring of her heart, she remained as still as a statue. Andy hurried to her side and offered her a congratulatory hug; Mira and Lina gathered to join them. "God has done great things in you, my little one," said Mira.

"Only because you were there to catch me. To God goes the glory of moving at a snail's pace," laughed Bella.

"I've always known God has His reasons for my pace," chuckled Mira. "I think the crowd would like to hear more from you. Do you think you can shine a little bit more for them?"

At Mira's insistence, Bella brought the gathering back into a reflection. "It's no mistake that I am here today, surrounded by God's beauty. I can feel the warmth of the Holy Spirit within me and surrounding all of you. My preparation for this new journey has taught me how to see God in the little things."

Just then, Bella began to flutter higher in the air. Her wings shone with all the colors of the rainbow. Each color had crystallized, giving the appearance of stained glass. The sight of Bella was spectacular and one which no one would ever forget. Her confidence had changed her appearance, making her brighter than she'd ever been.

"God has called me into ministry, and in the presence of you all, I answer yes!" she shouted. Bella then lifted her gaze to the sky. "Lord, You held me in my chrysalis until I was confident and ready to surrender to You. In losing my old self and becoming a new creation,[17] I now can use this gift for Your greater good." Suddenly, Bella flew all around the pond, leaving a trail of stardust with every flutter of her wings.

"Look at her go!" shouted Mira.

"She's radiant!" exclaimed Dottie.

"Absolutely glowing!" cheered Gracie.

As they watched Bella soar through the sky, her light glittering on the surface of the water, Dottie let out a sigh. "I think this goodbye is going to be harder than most," said Dottie.

"This is not goodbye," Mira responded. "It's a wonderful new beginning, one in which they will both go, grow, and glow!" Bella looked magical as she flew all around her friends, and a celebration of faith and gratitude towards God continued well into the night.

As the moon took its place in the night sky, Mira and Bella snuck off for a private chat. "I know what's coming," said Bella.

"You've got to spread your wings," Mira responded.

"There has to be a way you can fly with me," said Bella. "You carried me all that time. Let me carry you for a while."

"Even if I had my own wings for flight, I could not accompany you this time. God has designed this part of your journey to be traveled without me," responded Mira.

"Oh, but I can't leave you!" Bella cried out.

"Hush now, little one. You are embarking on one of the biggest adventures of your new life," said Mira.

"I don't see how anything could be bigger than this last adventure," replied Bella. "However, I know never to underestimate the power of God!"

"Look over there," said Mira as she gestured toward a branch, where Lina and Andy had perched.

"They are saying their farewells too, aren't they?" asked Bella.

"Not farewell, my dear. They are saying hello to the unknown. In doing so, they are accepting the change God has asked for and will embrace it in complete surrender."

"I remember how worried I was about transformation and change," remarked Bella. "However, with you and the others, the thought of change is kind of exciting. I can do this! I can do all things with God!"

Mira and Bella spent a few more moments with one another with the knowledge that they would see one another soon. When the time was right, Bella and Andy positioned themselves for flight at the top of the waterfall.

"This is it! The road to our new beginning!" exclaimed Andy. "Ready! Set! Go!"

"I will always remember the gift of your friendships," Bella shouted as she flew high and into the clouds. Andy did not hesitate to follow.

"Be glad and enjoy God's fruit!" he cheered as he fluttered away.

Bella and Andy flew gracefully out of the meadow and through the forest. God guided them through whispers in the breeze. Resting often on the journey gave Andy ample time to fill his tummy. All the while, Bella admired her reflection in every puddle or pond possible. They traveled together for quite some time before Andy felt an urge that God needed him elsewhere. "I feel a little different today," he said.

"How so?" questioned Bella.

"All of a sudden, I have a fire in my belly to study more of God's Word. I can't put this book down. It's making it difficult to keep up with our travels."

"Have you prayed and asked God for direction?" she asked.

"I have, and I'm sure that God is calling me to a new path, separate from yours. God sends me to pages in His Word that are telling me it is time for us to part," Andy replied.

"If God is giving you insights, then that's what you must do," said Bella. "Each of us should use the gifts we have received to serve others."

At that, Andy's mouth fell open, and he tore open his book to a worn-out page. "See this?" he asked. "I've been reading this page over and over again and praying about it every day to see what God wants me to do with it. You! Bella! You have given me a sign that God indeed sent me to this page."

"I haven't seen you this excited since we gained our wings," said Bella. "Please continue."

"Here, just read what I have marked," Andy said as he handed the page to Bella.

"First Peter 4:10. It says, 'Each of you should use whatever gift you have received to serve others.'"[18] Bella's voice trailed off at the end when she realized what Andy was trying to show her.

"See that! God put His words into your mouth! Words from the page I have been praying with!" said Andy.

"Why are you so surprised?" asked Bella. "God's blessings are nothing to sneeze at! Consider this a God-kissed moment. Accept it and enjoy everything it will offer you. This is our time now to go and feed God's little children."

At that, Bella allowed herself to well up with blessed tears and said her goodbyes to her dear friend. "I am sad, but I am confident our paths will cross again," said Bella.

"What about you?" asked Andy.

"Now that you mention it, I've been praying with a page from God's Word as well," Bella replied.

"Oh, exciting! Where is God leading you?" Andy asked.

"Home," said Bella. "God's Word is leading me home."

"I know that God will bless you on your journey," Andy said with a smile, "and you will be a wonderful gift to someone very special."

At that moment, Andy's wings opened wide, and he flew toward his new adventure. Feeling a sudden urge to flutter her wings herself, Bella kissed a prayer to God before taking flight. "God, when I feel lost, help me to trust You to lead me on the path toward home. Amen."

Now accustomed to her new form, Bella fluttered high among the clouds. Using God's breath in the breeze to guide her, she traveled with confidence and excitement for her future. Bella thought about many things while she flew around the forest. She often found herself asking God what was to come next, but she delighted in the hope of surprises along her way.

One day, while she was enjoying the peacefulness of her surroundings, Bella spotted a dusty-looking butterfly with a broken wing on the ground below. As she looked upon it, she experienced a sense of familiarity. Upon her approach, she considered a passage from the cave of blessings. However, wanting to make sure she remembered it correctly, Bella reached for her Bible.

This time, as she touched the page, a childhood memory came upon her. She could see her grandmother holding a Bible illuminated by light. In this vision, Bella was seated at her side with eyes full of child-like faith. *I must be awfully close to home,* she thought. *God has revealed the seed planted in me all those years ago.*

Silently, Bella thanked God for such a lovely memory and asked Him to place the words into her heart.

As Bella approached the path, the light surrounding her intensified, so much so that the broken butterfly could not see Bella's face. "Hello, I'm Bella," she introduced herself. "It's nice to have found you." The broken butterfly gazed silently into Bella's light.

Having gotten no response, Bella continued. "You must not be afraid. I was sent to find you." This still did not provoke any reaction from the broken butterfly. Bella quickly devised a plan and grabbed hold of a large leaf from a nearby tree. Positioning herself under the leaf cast a shadow upon her and the little butterfly. As the shadow fell upon them, they both looked at each other in awe.

"Are you okay?" Bella asked. Captivated by Bella's appearance, the broken butterfly was speechless and simply gestured a yes by nodding her head.

"You look very familiar to me," said Bella. "Let me get a good look at you." At that, Bella inched closer. At first glance, Bella saw something in the broken butterfly that reminded her of the day she landed on Mira. Bella's heart warmed, and a gentle breeze held her close. *God is here*, she thought.

Memories of that special day swiftly took over Bella's mind. Hearing Mira's voice echo within her, Bella paused to recall Mira's words. "God led me to you by putting me on your path. You are my big thing!" Knowing this moment was a precious gift, Bella kissed a prayer up to God.

"I am Mirabella," the butterfly finally replied, bringing Bella's gaze back to the path. Hearing that name should have surprised Bella; however, knowing that this butterfly was a gift from God, it was not much of a shock.

"My, what a beautiful miracle you are," said Bella.

"I'm not feeling very beautiful," replied Mirabella. "I was flying, and I snagged my wing on a branch. After that, I was not strong enough to fly. I landed on this path, rolled a bit, and now I am covered in dust. I must be quite the sight."

"Indeed you are!" exclaimed Bella. "I've never seen anything more beautiful." Bella's statement brought confusion to Mirabella, and several questions popped into her mind and out of her mouth.

"You must need glasses," said Mirabella. "Any chance you know how to fix a broken wing? Maybe there is a pond around where I could clean the dust off? Why are you surrounded by so much light?"

Bella was amused at how much Mirabella reminded her of herself. Knowing that she needed to provide reassurance, Bella snuggled close to her. "Come, little one," she said. "You look like you could use a little God-time."

ENDNOTES

Life is a journey, the circumstances of which affect each one individually. A common thread among all is God's Spirit within us. Included here are Bella's lessons for reflection. These may be helpful in prayer, Bible study, group discussion, or family conversations. Bearing in mind that each insight may hold a different meaning for us all, and we will "get out of it" what God intends. I hope you delight in each one as you seek God's truth and wisdom planted within its fruit.

Trust the journey.

Tears are healing.

Learn how to look for and be open to God's blessings.

Listen for God's call.

Prayers are often answered in unimaginable ways.

God turns darkness into light.

God's strength is always with us.

Believe that God makes things beautiful.

God turns scars into beautiful masterpieces.

Those who walk in God's light are called to share His love and good news.

God will provide food for the journey; be open to feed upon it.

Trust in your faith, and God will lead you close to Him.

When patience is needed, rest in God's presence.

Be strong and of good courage.

Prayer and God's strength will get you through anything.

1. Psalm 32:8 (NLT).
2. 1 John 2:8 (NOG).
3. John 8:12 (RSV).
4. Psalm 119:105 (ESV).
5. Joshua 1:9 (ESV).
6. Joshua 1:9 (NKJV).
7. Psalm 18:2 (KJV).
8. 2 Corinthians 5:7 (NRSV).
9. See Luke 1:37 (ESV).
10. 2 Corinthians 5:7 (ESV).
11. Philippians 4:13 (NKJV).
12. See Ephesians 1:18 (RSV).
13. John 1:39 (NKJV).
14. See Matthew 19:26 (NLT).
15. John 12:46 (RSV).
16. Psalm 56:3 (NIV).
17. See 2 Corinthians 5:17 (NIV).
18. 1 Peter 4:10 (NIV).

ABOUT THE AUTHOR

Bella's Beautiful Miracle is Kimberly's first published work based on a series of life events and treasured friendships. This story, though fictional, is a reflection of many pivotal moments on Kimberly's journey of finding God in all things. Kimberly may not have been a caterpillar who landed upon a snail; rather, she followed the leading of the Holy Spirit, embraced her child-like faith, and gave life to Bella's Journey.

Kimberly Novak is a child of God, wife, mother, author, and spiritual director. Her calling to minister to the spiritual needs of others was born when sudden changes developed in her personal life. Embracing the gift in those struggles allowed God to mold and transform her in ways that enable her to help those around her. Kimberly's mission is to enhance each journey by guiding others where the light of strength is…God's love.